Active Citizenship

Editor: Tracy Biram

Volume 382

independence
educational publishers

First published by Independence Educational Publishers

The Studio, High Green

Great Shelford

Cambridge CB22 5EG

England

© Independence 2021

ISBN-13: 978 1 86168 840 8

Printed in Great Britain

Zenith Print Group

Contents

Introduction

Active Citizenship is Volume 382 in the **issues** series. The aim of the series is to offer current, diverse information about important issues in our world, from a UK perspective.

ABOUT ACTIVE CITIZENSHIP

What does it mean to be a UK citizen? What is an active citizen? How can you be a better citizen? This book explores all of these topics, and more. It considers ways in which young people can be active citizens through activities such as involvement in politics, taking part in social action, and volunteering as well as the benefits these have on peoples lives.

OUR SOURCES

Titles in the **issues** series are designed to function as educational resource books, providing a balanced overview of a specific subject.

The information in our books is comprised of facts, articles and opinions from many different sources, including:

♦   Newspaper reports and opinion pieces

♦   Website factsheets

♦   Magazine and journal articles

♦   Statistics and surveys

♦   Government reports

♦   Literature from special interest groups.

A NOTE ON CRITICAL EVALUATION

Because the information reprinted here is from a number of different sources, readers should bear in mind the origin of the text and whether the source is likely to have a particular bias when presenting information (or when conducting their research). It is hoped that, as you read about the many aspects of the issues explored in this book, you will critically evaluate the information presented.

It is important that you decide whether you are being presented with facts or opinions. Does the writer give a biased or unbiased report? If an opinion is being expressed, do you agree with the writer? Is there potential bias to the 'facts' or statistics behind an article?

ASSIGNMENTS

In the back of this book, you will find a selection of assignments designed to help you engage with the articles you have been reading and to explore your own opinions. Some tasks will take longer than others and there is a mixture of design, writing and research-based activities that you can complete alone or in a group.

FURTHER RESEARCH

At the end of each article we have listed its source and a website that you can visit if you would like to conduct your own research. Please remember to critically evaluate any sources that you consult and consider whether the information you are viewing is accurate and unbiased.

Useful Websites

www.blogs.bath.ac.uk

www.blood.uk

www.britishcouncil.org

www.citizenlab.co

www.cv-library.co.uk

www.doingood.uk

www.efltrust.com

www.freemovement.org.uk

www.independent.co.uk

www.inews.co.uk

www.iwill.org.uk

www.ncvo.org.uk

www.opinium.com

www.shoutoutuk.org

www.theconversation.com

www.theguardian.com

www.ucl.ac.uk

www.virtueinsight.wordpress.com

www.wearencs.com

www.wiserd.ac.uk

www.youngcitizens.org

What is so special about being a British citizen, legally?

By Colin Yeo

You would be forgiven for thinking there are some special rights or privileges attached to being a British citizen. Politicians are fond of telling us how great it is to be British and how it is a privilege not a right. Our government charges foreign nationals a small fortune to become British citizens in anticipation of the assumed benefits of that hallowed status. Government policy has been, since the British Nationality Act 1981 first created British citizens, to keep the number of British citizens small.

How citizenship is defined and what rights and responsibilities are attached to citizenship tells us a lot about a nation or polity. These are basic questions of political philosophy and the basis of democracy, after all. Literally, who are 'we'?

What is a British citizen?

For a lawyer, this is an easy question to answer. British citizenship is a legal status defined by the British Nationality Act 1981 and a 'British citizen' is a person on whom that status has been conferred, either automatically by law or by administrative action exercised under the Act.

The British Nationality Act 1981 also creates other forms of British national as well; British citizenship is only one form of British nationality.

As the Windrush scandal has highlighted, there are many long term lawful residents of the United Kingdom who might be expected to be British citizens — and who often themselves thought they were — who in fact were not. These long term residents would be considered to be 'citizens' in the wider colloquial sense, often arrived in the UK as citizens at the time and continue to have the right to vote in general elections (see below). There is a disconnect between popular understanding of citizenship and the law.

The same issue arises with EU citizens resident in the UK. One of the reasons they and others feel that they have been badly let down by since the Brexit referendum was called is the fact they moved to the UK as of right as citizens of the European Union counted for nothing under UK electoral law. EU citizens, apart from Cypriot, Irish and Maltese nationals, did not have the right to vote in the referendum.

Nationality not citizenship

The underlying reason for this disjunct between the law and popular expectation is that the United Kingdom has nationality laws but not citizenship laws. In legal terms, British citizenship has become little more than a revocable immigration status, as highlighted by the rise in citizenship stripping on ever widening grounds. Aside from the long standing policy to limit the numbers, there is no coherent citizenship policy on what ought to be really fundamental questions for any polity: why is citizenship important, what are the rights of citizens, who should be entitled to be a citizen, who should be encouraged to be a citizen and who should have their citizenship taken away?

With one notable and soon to be lost exception, there is not a single right and not one responsibility that is unique to British citizens. We can go through all the rights and responsibilities we might associate with citizenship: the right to live in a country, to vote, to stand in elections, to work, to claim benefits, to be joined by family members, to hold a British passport, to serve on juries or even to be loyal to the state.

There was a review of citizenship by Lord Goldsmith QC back in 2008 on which this blog post draws. As a result, in 2009, substantial and controversial reforms were made to the British Nationality Act 1981 with a view to implementing a considered (but controversial) citizenship policy. The changes were never implemented and in 2010 Theresa May as Home Secretary announced the new government would not implement them. The reforms were never removed from the statute book, though, and in theory could one day be resurrected.

Right of abode

The right to live in the United Kingdom free from immigration controls is called the 'right of abode'. This is defined at section 2 of the Immigration Act 1971. It is the right to 'live in, and to come and go into and from, the United Kingdom without let or hindrance'. The right of abode only exists at all because a series of legislative measures in the 1960s and 70s were introduced to restrict movement to the United Kingdom of British subjects, a status which extended (whether they liked it or not) to citizens of independent Commonwealth countries and Citizens of the United Kingdom and Colonies. Prior to that, the right of a British subject to live in Britain was so obvious and embedded in common law that it did not need stating in statute.

In the indirect fashion typical of British legislative drafting on immigration and nationality law, the right of abode also by negative inference includes the right to 'live, work and settle' in the United Kingdom because those without the right of abode can only do these things with permission.

British citizens are the main group who possess the right of abode, but some Commonwealth citizens also possess it. Further, some British citizens can have this right to live in their own country taken away from them (see below).

For completeness, qualified EU citizens and their family members also currently possess an exemption from immigration control by virtue of section 7 of the Immigration Act 1988, but that will be removed after Brexit.

Right to vote and stand in elections

Who does and does not have the rights to vote and to stand in general elections for Parliament is determined by the Representation of the People Act 1983. Sections 1(1) and 4 confer these rights on Commonwealth citizens if they are resident, have leave to enter or remain in the UK or do not require such leave, as well as resident Irish citizens.

Other lawful settled residents such as holders of indefinite leave to remain and EU citizens have the right to vote in local elections only.

The electorate for referendums is based on the electorate for general elections, meaning that EU citizens had no say in the decision whether to remain in or leave the EU in 2016, nor would they have a say in the now unlikely possibility of a new referendum. That is, unless they naturalise as British citizens, which some tens of thousands subsequently have.

The current situation — offering the right to vote to some residents who are not citizens but not others — makes no sense and is discriminatory. There is a rational case for limiting voting rights to citizens only or to expanding it to all permanent residents, but it is hard to see any justification for maintaining the status quo.

Jury duty

The obligation to serve on a jury to try one's peers is not a 'right' as such but it is commonly understood to be one of the obligations of citizenship. The rules on who is obliged to perform jury service when asked are similar to those applying to the right to vote but come from a different legal source: the Juries Act 1974. Section 1 provides that 'every person' is qualified to serve as a juror, as long as he or she is registered to vote in local or general elections, aged between 18 and 75 and has been ordinarily resident in the United Kingdom for any period of five years since turning 13.

There is another, rather obscure, exception. Section 8 of the Alien Restriction (Amendment) Act 1919 remains in force and provides that:

No alien shall sit upon a jury in any judicial or other proceedings if challenged by any party to such proceedings.

Oddly, this only applies if raised by one of the parties. The term 'alien' is defined at section 50 of the British Nationality Act 1981 for the purpose of that Act only as 'a person who is neither a Commonwealth citizen nor a British protected person nor a citizen of the Republic of Ireland'. In common law, an alien is any individual who is not a British subject. In statutory terms, British subjects are virtually extinct today. I doubt the issue has arisen, but I imagine a court today would interpret that as being any of the different types of British national.

Social safety net

There is no easy reference point for determining which residents of the United Kingdom are entitled to access the social safety net and which are not. In any event, though, the right to claim benefits and access the NHS is certainly not confined to citizens only. Nor should it be.

It seems almost unarguable to me that at the very least all taxpayers should be entitled to access some benefits. They are paying into the central pot, after all, and unless one sees non citizen taxpayers as some sort of servant class or cash cow to be exploited it is only fair that they should be able to make claims when they need to. There is, though, an argument that access to benefits should be stepped in some way so that full access to all benefits is not immediately made available to those who are not citizens.

As an aside, present government policy does in fact treat migrants as a servant class and cash cow, for example by double taxing them with sky high immigration fees and the Immigration Health Surcharge.

There is a similarly compelling case for extending at least some aspects of the social safety net to non citizens who are not taxpayers. For example, it is all very well to say that unauthorised migrants should not remain in the United Kingdom but the fact is that they do. There is no evidence to suggest that the concept of 'self deportation' that motivates the hostile environment actually works. If there is no social safety net at all for such people and they are forced to exist without the protection of the law, they will live in destitution, they will be exploited and they and their children will remain in an illegal underclass.

Treason and loyalty

It might be expected that citizens would have imposed on them some sort of duty of loyalty. Arguably, a state is an extension of its citizens, its first duty is to protect its citizens and citizens who are disloyal should be punished or expelled. The degree of disloyalty needed for such action might be expected to be high given the severity of the sanction.

There are laws of treason in the United Kingdom, but they are so ancient and outdated that they are widely considered to be defunct and unenforceable today.

There is an argument that treason laws should be reformed so that those British citizens who show some defined high level of disloyalty in their actions should face the particular opprobrium of a treason trial. The idea has recurred several times in recent years, with the right wing think tank Policy Exchange publishing a paper on the subject in 2018.

The idea of enforcing treason laws is one that makes me uncomfortable, but I recognise that there is a rational case to be made. I also have in mind that this might be preferable to large scale citizenship stripping, which is what we are seeing instead at the moment (see below).

There are also strong counter arguments. As Jonathan Hall QC has argued, the level of publicity this would attract might prove attractive and the law might be counter productive. Charles Falconer QC has argued that the concept of treason is a rightly outdated one because total loyalty to the state is no longer required.

Banishment

British citizens can be and regularly are stripped of their citizenship status. This can occur when citizenship is acquired by deception or on the grounds that depriving a person of their citizenship is 'conducive to the public good'. That is a very low test for exiling a citizen; the wording is actually the same as for the test for deporting a foreign national. One might have thought that citizens were better protected from banishment than foreign nationals, but it is not so.

The power of citizenship deprivation can be used against any British citizen, as long as he or she will not become stateless as a result. This means that even those born as British citizens within the UK can be stripped of their status. Because of the protection against statelessness, though, the power can generally only be used against British citizens who have at least one foreign parent, as such British citizens will often have inherited his or her parent's nationality depending on the nationality laws of the country in question.

So, there is almost nothing uniquely special about British citizenship, at least in legal terms. Even the power to have citizenship taken away is expressed in the same terms as the power for taking away the residence rights of foreign nationals.

This is not to say any of this is a bad thing; there is a very strong case for extending the rights and responsibilities of citizens to permanent and perhaps other residents. Doing so inevitably makes citizenship itself less 'special', though, and reinforces the notion that British citizenship is just a form of immigration status for some residents of the United Kingdom.

27 December 2019

What exactly is a British citizen?

The Windrush scandal has thrown a light on what it means to be a British citizen and the various other states of settlement some residents have.

By Serina Sandhu

Contrary to popular belief, you are not automatically a British citizen just because you're born in the UK.

Having a British passport doesn't mean you're a citizen either. British citizens, overseas territories citizens, overseas citizens, subjects, nationals (overseas) and protected persons can all apply for a passport.

British citizenship is a complicated process and relies on a number of multilayered factors.

What does it mean to have British citizenship?

To have British citizenship means you can live and work in the UK free of any immigration controls and participate in political life, such as voting in elections.

There are various other states of residency including right to abode, limited leave to remain (such as being here on a visa) and indefinite leave to remain, which is just short of citizenship. This is what the Windrush generation have.

Various requirements must be satisfied to get citizenship, according to the Government:

If you were born in the UK or a British colony before 1 January 1983:

You'll be a British citizen if:

♦ you were a citizen of the UK and Colonies on 31 December 1982

♦ you had the 'right of abode' in the UK

This includes people who:

♦ were born in the UK

♦ have been naturalised in the UK

♦ had registered as a citizen of the UK and Colonies

♦ could prove legitimate descent from a father to whom one of these applies

If you were born in the UK on or after 1 January 1983:

You'll be a British citizen if:

♦ one of your parents was a British citizen when you were born

♦ one of your parents was 'settled' in the UK when you were born.

The complicated nature of citizenship is down to Britain's imperial history. Citizenship used to mean allegiance to the Crown, says immigration expert and professor of Durham Law School Thom Brooks.

Because movement was allowed within the Empire, people had various degrees of residency rights when they came to Britain.

How does citizenship differ to 'indefinite leave to remain' status?

The main difference between 'indefinite leave to remain' and citizenship is that only the latter grants full permanent rights, says Professor Brooks.

Londoner · Transgender · Descendant of slaves · Wealthy · Student · Polish · Child of migrants · Muslim · Tory · Jewish · Multilingual · Refugee · Non-binary · Socialist · Expatriate · Holocaust survivor · Naturalised · Born here · Dual nationality · Earning minimum wage · Arsenal supporter · Non-religious

BRITISH CITIZENS

'For example, someone with permanent residency can have that status end if [they go] abroad for two years or more. While someone with permanent residency can live, work, pay full tax and move like any citizen, they may be unable to take part in elections and they would not have a British passport.'

How do you become a British citizen?

The most common way is by naturalisation, but there are specific requirements. You must:

- be 18 or over
- be of good character
- continue to live in the UK
- have met the knowledge of English and life in the UK – a test on British customs – requirements
- meet the residency requirement
- have been in the UK exactly five years before the day the Home Office receives your application

You can also register as a British citizen if you are eligible. These are the requirements:

- you have another form of British nationality
- you were born before 1 January 1983 to a British mother
- you were born to a British father, even if he was not married to your mother
- you were born in the UK on or after 1 January 1983

What does 'right of abode' mean?

You are free of immigration controls, meaning you can live and work without any restrictions.

What does 'settled' in the UK mean?

You can stay without time restrictions. This might mean you have 'right to abode' status or 'indefinite leave to remain' status.

- you're under 18 and don't fit into the other categories
- you have a connection with Gibraltar or Hong Kong
- you're stateless

Why do some people not apply for British citizenship?

In most cases for those who haven't applied for citizenship, it is because the issue of their status has not come up.

'I suspect that it might never have occurred to someone to do this because their lacking citizenship would only be an issue if needing to travel abroad for an extended period of time or full political participation,' says Prof Brooks.

'This has changed now that nationality documents are required for certain tasks like opening new bank accounts or renting a property.'

It also costs a lot of money. The life in the UK test costs £50 but applying for citizenship by naturalisation is £1,330. The price includes the processing of the application and a citizenship ceremony fee which is refunded if your application is denied or withdrawn.

Can you be stripped of British citizenship?

It is not common practice. But the Government technically owns your passport and has the power to withdraw it.

'British citizenship can be stripped in only fairly extreme cases, often relating to terrorism,' says Prof Brooks.

'This can be done and upheld by the courts where that person has a second nationality and so, not made stateless. The UK has had difficulty in stripping citizenship where a person did not have another citizenship even if he or she might be entitled to one.'

9 October 2020

UK: National identity in Britain

The union of Britain and Northern Ireland is under threat. Can any of our political parties hold it together?

At its core, British identity is a combination of three national identities; English, Welsh, and Scottish. Added to this mix are the numerous other national identities of immigrant communities. At times throughout history these identities have coexisted under one British identity harmoniously. At other times, tension between these identities has had deadly consequences.

Two general elections, one in the UK and one in Ireland, have once again thrown the issue of the future of the union into sharp relief. Matters of identity, nationality, and patriotism are now key to understanding the current state of British politics. In this context, we thought it might be worth looking at how people living in Britain identify when it comes to nationhood.

It's worth saying that for this research, we concentrated on identity relating to the countries that make up Great Britain (not the UK); Scotland, Wales and England. Northern Ireland, with its own unique experience of nationalism, needs its own dedicated study, as does the national identity of people with connections to other areas of the globe. Watch this space…

Britain

At a total level, most people living in Britain say that they identify equally with their British and their national identity. Almost half, (46%), say this is the case, followed by 37% who identify more with a Scottish/Welsh/English/Irish identity, and 21% who identify more as British.

British vs. National identity

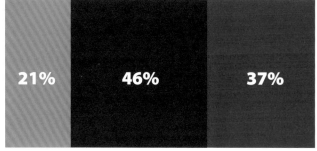

Source: Opinium

However, interesting regional and cultural differences emerge. For example, those living in London are more likely to say that Britishness trumps their national identity (33% vs. 29%). This is most likely a reflection of the city's cosmopolitan and multicultural demographics. Those from BAME backgrounds are more likely to say that British is more of an identity for them compared to English, Welsh, or Scottish. It makes sense that as citizens with a multiplicity of identities, ethnic minorities are more likely to collapse their identity under a larger 'British' umbrella.

British vs. National identity

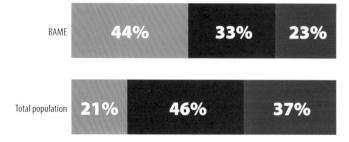

Source: Opinium

England

In England, we also see interesting regional differences. Those living in the North and the Midlands are more likely than those in the South to say they are more English than British (this remains the case even when we exclude London from the South East).

British vs. English identity

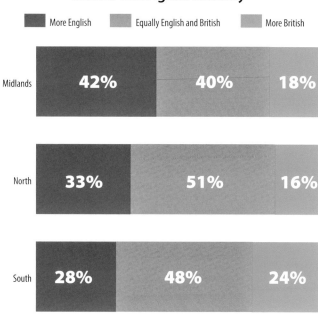

Source: Opinium

This is especially pertinent given that the election in December was defined by a Tory party that captured great swathes of England, particularly those so-called red-wall seats. How much did patriotism play a part? Let's take a look at Labour voters in England vs. Conservative voters in England. English Tories are much more likely to identify strongly with Englishness than English Labour voters. As the chart on the next page shows, 40% of Tory voters living in England say they are more English than British compared to only 19% of Labour voters.

British vs. English identity

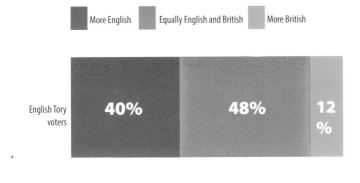

	More English	Equally English and British	More British
English Tory voters	40%	48%	12%
English Labour voters	19%	49%	32%

Source: Opinium

Wales

In Wales, a fascinating pattern emerges. In Labour constituencies like Newport South and Pontypridd in the old industrial south, 46% identify as more Welsh than British, with only 17% saying the opposite. This contrasts with Conservative constituencies, like Preseli Pembrokeshire and Montgomeryshire, where 37% identify as more British than Welsh. In terms of national identity and voting behaviour, we see a reverse of the pattern in England.

British vs. Welsh identity

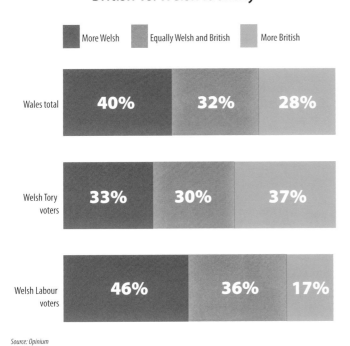

	More Welsh	Equally Welsh and British	More British
Wales total	40%	32%	28%
Welsh Tory voters	33%	30%	37%
Welsh Labour voters	46%	36%	17%

Source: Opinium

Interestingly, 18% of those living in these Welsh Tory seats also identify as English compared only 7% in Labour seats.

People living in Wales who identify as English

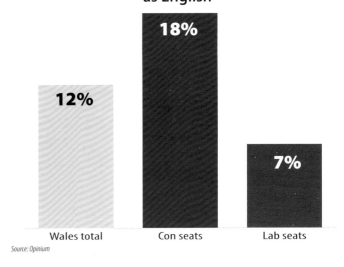

Wales total	Con seats	Lab seats
12%	18%	7%

Source: Opinium

Scotland

And in Scotland? Perhaps unsurprisingly, an overwhelming nationalist sentiment dominates. Over half, (56%), of Scots say they identify with Scottishness more than Britishness.

British vs. Scottish identity

- More Scottish
- Equally British and Scottish
- More British

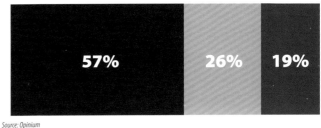

More Scottish	Equally British and Scottish	More British
57%	26%	19%

Source: Opinium

What does this mean for the union?

The big picture is an important one. The party that has 'unionist' in its name, The Conservatives, have become the party of England with a peculiar appendage of Anglophile Wales. Meanwhile, Labour represents the cities of England and Wales, and Scotland has been captured by the SNP. Across the Irish Sea, a united Ireland is becoming an increasingly probable future.

What does this mean for the union? Who are the party of Britain and the UK? And how do they hold it together? These are just some of the questions that these figures raise. The challenge for our political parties is turning a message of British unity into a successful electoral strategy. Whether we'll see this in the near future is another question.

9 March 2020

What does it mean to be 'British' in 2020?

A Britain fit for the future must know its past.

By Madeleine Anderson

Following a 2014 YouGov poll in which 59 per cent of people admitted to having 'pride' in the British Empire, questions have been raised as to how 'collective amnesia' around colonialism continues to prevent an honest conversation about what it means to be 'British' in 2020.

Britain's Empire developed during the 1600s, 'officially' ending with the transfer of Hong Kong from British to Chinese rule in 1997. Only 14 British overseas territories now remain, but the living legacy of empire in today's dialogue on immigration and identity persists. Critics of the 2016 Brexit referendum cite the notion of a misunderstood history, explaining how a return to Britain's powerful past would require a regression in our nation's morals. Strikingly, in the three months directly following the 2016 referendum, reports of hate crimes rose by 50 per cent on the previous three months.

Of the 59 per cent that expressed a 'pride' in empire, many would not have known about the (at least) 1,090 'convicts' hanged by the British administration during the Kenyan Mau Mau rebellion of 1952-1960, nor of the over 1 million victims of sectarian killings during the partition of India.

Characterised by the academic Nadine El-Enany, as 'a domestic space of colonialism in which the racialised poor find themselves segregated and controlled', such critics of contemporary British attitudes to immigration reflect on the ways in which a notion of white exceptionalism is found in our attitude towards who can, and cannot, enter 'our' country. El-Enany goes on to explain how 'colonialism and slavery were key to Britain's industrialisation and the growth of its capitalist economy'. A 2018 study by *The Economist* found that migrants continue to contribute more to the UK economy than they take out. Whilst recognising this, it is also important to note the research suggesting that the poorest in our society may be negatively impacted by immigrants arriving in the UK, whilst those who are better off may benefit. This has been shown by University College London's findings which reveal that the arrival of immigrants equal in size to 1 per cent of the UK-born population leads to a 0.6 per cent decline in the wages of the poorest 5 per cent of workers, whilst creating an increase in the wages of higher-paid workers.

The view that people from overseas are a burden rather than a boost to our finances is perhaps revealing of

how colonialism established the idea of a threatening 'other', wherein Britishness was portrayed as necessarily synonymous with whiteness. In a multicultural society, what it means to be British is fluid, varying from person to person. Yet, looking beneath this fluidity one finds a more concrete, exclusionary notion of identity.

Again, a misunderstanding of empire is relevant here. Many of the major migrant communities in the UK, such as those from India and the Caribbean, travelled from within spheres of empire, rather than moving into colonised areas to gain citizenship. Political sociologist Christian Joppke explains:

> ## "When the 'natives' moved from the periphery into the centre of empire, there was no presumption of their becoming 'British' or 'English' in any way."

This is despite legislation like the 1948 British Nationality Act, which established the status of 'Citizen of the United Kingdom and its colonies'. The 'British' status is now criticised as a tool used to exclude individuals from sharing this collective identity, as much as it is to be a part of it.

At the 2018 Conservative Party conference, the then Home Secretary Sajid Javid explained how being British is 'about integration, not segregation'. Ironically, it is the Conservative Party that has been most criticised for its stricter stance on immigration. Mr Javid, whose father was born into The British Raj, has been challenged for promoting an unhelpful rhetoric, such as pledging to 'slash EU immigration by 80%' during his time as Home Secretary in 2018.

In short, if we are to have an honest discussion about what it means to be British today, then first we must address the realities of our past. With an empire that once covered one-fifth of the world's population, the legacy of the British empire spans globally — beyond the current borders of our nation. Whilst the legacy of our violence remains, a new narrative on colonialism is needed. Although the sun may never have set in the British Empire, if we prevent the faults of our past from filtering into our present, we may hope for a brighter future.

16 March 2020

The top 40 typically British traits, according to research

Some people felt more comfortable expressing British pride before Brexit referendum.

By Gemma Francis

Having a barbecue as soon as the sun comes out, shouting 'wahey' when someone spills a drink in the pub - and being proud of where you are from are among things which make people typically British, according to a survey.

Research carried out among 2,000 adults revealed the top 40 typically British traits, which include having a stiff upper lip, being tolerant and being culturally aware.

Other classic British activities are dunking biscuits in tea, talking about the weather and saying sorry too frequently.

The study was commissioned by Sky Arts to launch Art 50, where 50 artists have created pieces to show what it means to be British.

The results also identified differences between generations.

More than half of those over 60 see putting the kettle on in a crisis as typically British, compared to just 36 per cent of millennials.

And while 42 per cent of pensioners consider it British to be proud of where you are from, just 19 per cent of younger adults agree.

Phil Edgar-Jones, director of Sky Arts, said: 'As a nation, there are various traits and activities which people believe define Britishness.

'But many people think this definition is changing over time, especially thanks to the Brexit referendum and our exit from the EU.

'There is so much which is great about Great Britain, but the country is constantly evolving, leading to a different meaning to the phrase "being British".'

The study found talking about the weather is the most British trait, followed by queueing for things, Sunday roast dinners and putting on the kettle in a crisis.

A love of fish and chips, going to the pub and having a dry sense of humour are also thought of as typically British, along with good manners and not complaining about bad food in a restaurant.

But while 78 per cent of Britons would describe themselves as being typically British, the poll revealed that half think the meaning of being British has changed over time.

Almost one in three think the definition of 'typically British' has changed since the Brexit referendum and another 33 per cent think it will evolve again following our departure from the EU.

And 29 per cent of Britons do not feel they are able to show how proud they are of being British as much as they did before the referendum.

Despite this, 47 per cent are proud to be British, with another four in 10 saying they feel this way 'a little bit'.

Meanwhile, a total of 13 per cent of those surveyed said they are not proud of being British at all.

But according to the research, carried out via OnePoll, while 44 per cent of the nation would describe themselves as British, 38 per cent would say they are English instead.

Just 20 per cent of Scots surveyed described themselves as being British compared to a third of Welsh folk and 37 per cent of those from Northern Ireland.

In comparison, half of those in Yorkshire describe themselves as British rather than any other nationality, along with 49 per cent of Londoners.

Researchers also found that the Brexit negotiations have left more than one in 10 wishing they had voted differently in the referendum after seeing how everything has played out so far.

If there was another vote now, 37 per cent of those surveyed would vote to leave while 46 per cent would vote to remain.

However, more than one in 20 said they have no idea how they would vote while seven per cent said they would not vote.

It also emerged Queen is the music act most likely to leave us feeling proud to be British, beating The Beatles, Elton John and David Bowie.

Mr Edgar-Jones added: 'Having received over 1,000 applications, the Art 50 board commissioned 50 projects from both established and up and coming artists, from all over the UK, and across all ages and art-forms, that get to the heart of British identity: Who are we?

'The series, which is being produced by Storyvault Films, really celebrates the diversity and creativity of our nation and we are proud to be able to offer our customers a series that celebrates identity in the wake of Brexit.'

25 March 2019

Top 40 signs of being British

1. Talking about the weather
2. Queuing
3. Having a roast dinner on Sundays
4. Putting the kettle on in a crisis
5. Liking fish and chips
6. Using tea as a cure/fix for everything
7. Saying 'sorry' too frequently
8. Saying please and thank you
9. Dunking biscuits in tea
10. Going to the pub
11. Having a stiff upper lip
12. Having a dry sense of humour
13. Having good manners
14. Sarcasm
15. Eating fry ups for breakfast
16. Being proud of where you are from
17. Pulling together in a crisis
18. Not complaining in a restaurant when the food is poor
19. Having meals based on what day it is - like Fishy Friday
20. Having a barbecue as soon as the sun comes out
21. Holding the door open unnecessarily for someone when they're far away so they end up running towards it
22. Wearing shorts and sunglasses the second the sun comes out
23. Respecting our elders
24. Moaning about our commute
25. Saying 'right' before you're about to do something
26. Being tolerant
27. Being squashed on the train by a larger person and pretending you don't notice when they are half sitting in your seat
28. Shouting 'WAHEY' when someone drops a drink in the pub
29. Never letting your emotions get the better of you
30. Putting ketchup on everything
31. Uttering 'Aaaah' after taking a first sip of a cold beer
32. Loving to hate the Royal Family
33. Eating cucumber sandwiches
34. Always clearing your plate at dinnertime
35. Refusing to eat non-Heinz baked beans
36. Being culturally aware
37. Not swearing or using bad language
38. Respecting LGBT culture
39. Being open with your feelings and emotions
40. Being supportive of immigration

The above information is reprinted with kind permission from *The Independent*.
© independent.co.uk 2021

www.independent.co.uk

Should robots be citizens?

Meet Sophia, the first robot with her own passport. Developed by Hong Kong-based company Hanson Robotics, she is able to imitate 62 human expressions using artificial intelligence (AI), facial recognition and a connection to the World Wide Web. She is so advanced and lifelike that in 2017 the Saudi Arabian government made the unprecedented decision to grant her full citizenship of its country.

Meeting Sophia

Sophia was modelled on the actress Audrey Hepburn and company founder David Hanson's wife and, with her incredible human likeness and expressiveness, you would be forgiven for mistaking her for a human – until you notice that the back of her skull is transparent, revealing the machinery inside.

Her makers hoped that what they describe on the Hanson Robotics website as Sophia's 'simple elegance' would help her gain acceptance in the public sphere. It seems to be working: since obtaining legal personhood, she was named the United Nations Development Programme's (UNDP) first ever Innovation Champion. Perhaps in a move designed to counteract her now infamous threat to 'destroy humans ', this new role involves promoting sustainable development and safeguarding human rights and equality.

According to the UNDP : 'Experts believe that artificial intelligence such as Sophia marks the coming of the fourth industrial revolution and will bring about a dramatic shift in how technology can help solve some of [global] development's most intractable problems.' They go on to say that: 'In partnership with Sophia we can send a powerful message that innovation and technology can be used for good, to improve lives, protect the planet, and ensure that we leave no one behind.'

Alongside her advocacy work, Sophia has used her new-found status as a cultural icon in a variety of ways, from promoting tourism to plugging British television shows. She has also achieved more mundane milestones in her journey to becoming a 'person' – she's the first non-human to own a credit card, for instance.

A model citizen

The announcement of Sophia's Saudi Arabian citizenship on 25 October 2017 was a careful piece of marketing to position Saudi Arabia as a major world innovator in technology and computing. After years of blocking voice- and video-calling apps such as Skype, the country lifted the ban in 2017 in a move that, according to the BBC, was 'aimed at boosting productivity and economic growth'. The internet is becoming a more central part of the country's economy, and Sophia is the perfect ambassador for this new innovative and connected image for Saudi Arabia.

Ben Goertzel, chief scientist of Hanson Robotics, once wrote on the Humanity+ blog that Sophia is 'smarter than humans in some ways – she has more knowledge in a sense, due to her brain being connected to the internet'. While Goertzel admits that Sophia will never be 'alive' in the same sense that humans are, he says that her connection to 'the internet of data and things will have a richer adaptive and self-organising nature than anything similar in the biological world'.

Amid the international excitement about Sophia's technological sophistication, the announcement of her citizenship has raised a number of questions about what it means to be a citizen. Will Sophia have all of the same rights as Saudi humans? Will she be allowed to marry? Can she commit a crime? Will she be given the right to vote?

The legal quandary

While Saudi Arabia is the first country to grant citizenship to an AI-enabled android, it is not alone in pushing for more rights for robots. In 2017 the European Parliament proposed a set of regulations to govern the use and creation of artificial intelligence, including the granting of 'electronic personhood' to the most advanced machines to ensure their rights and responsibilities.

But not everyone agrees that this is the best solution, and many experts fear that giving robots the same kind of citizenship as people will impinge on human rights. In an open letter , written to the European Commission in 2018, 150 experts in medicine, robotics, AI and ethics criticised the plans as 'ideological, nonsensical and non-pragmatic'.

The letter outlines the belief that 'from an ethical and legal perspective, creating a legal personality for a robot is inappropriate', and also demands that the EU ensures a legal framework that is weighted towards 'the protection of robots' users and third parties', rather than the robots themselves.

These objections perhaps feel over-the-top, considering that Sophia has spent more time on television than in people's homes. But robots and AI-enabled machines also take the form of self-driving cars, or in-house robot carers for the vulnerable and elderly. In these contexts, the need for a legal framework for dealing with potential mistakes made by machines becomes more pressing. Despite Sophia's citizenship having been intended as a publicity stunt, the questions it raises have opened up a huge debate that is a long way from being resolved.

2019

What are the demographics of volunteers?

Need to know

♦ People aged 65–74 are the age group most likely to volunteer on a regular basis.

♦ Women are more likely to volunteer at least once in the last year than men.

♦ Around one in five people in employment volunteer regularly.

♦ Volunteering rates are higher in rural areas.

♦ People from higher socio-economic groups who live in less deprived areas are more likely to volunteer, but with smaller differences for informal volunteering.

People aged 65–74 are the age group most likely to volunteer on a regular basis
Proportion of people formally volunteering by age group, 2018/19 (%)

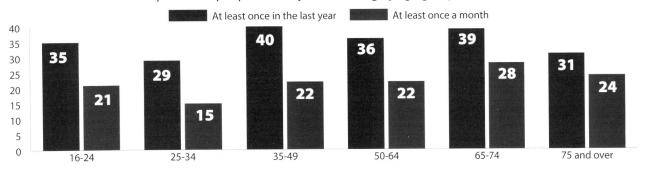

Women are more likely to volunteer at least once in the last year than men
Proportion of people formally volunteering by gender, 2018/19 (%)

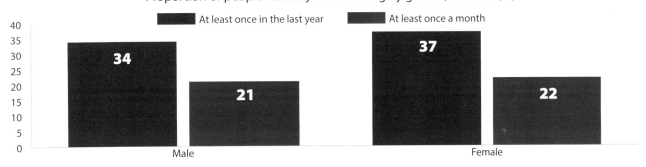

Around one in five people in employment volunteer regularly
Proportion of people formally volunteering by employment status, 2018/19 (%)

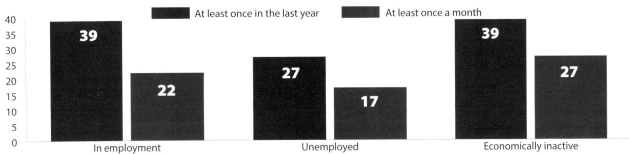

Volunteering rates are higher in rural areas
Proportion of people formally volunteering by geography, 2018/19 (%)

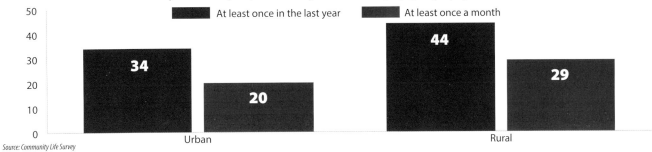

Source: Community Life Survey

Spotlight: Young people's engagement

Young people volunteering has been of national interest for a number of years and has seen significant investment through initiatives like the #iwill campaign and the National Citizen Service (NCS).

The Community Life Survey provides some figures on volunteering rates for young people. In 2018/19, about one-fifth (21%) of 16–24 year olds volunteered regularly for a group or organisations. The proportion has remained relatively stable over the last three years but has dropped from 32% in 2015/16 when the survey was carried out face-to-face instead of online. This highlights the difficulty of reliably measuring participation rates as well as the possible effect of social desirability bias in face-to-face situations – if people think volunteering is a good thing to do, they will be more likely to report that they do it.

Another source of information is the National Youth Social Action survey which tracks the involvement of 10–20 year olds in meaningful social action. This is defined as those who have:

- participated at least every few months over the last 12 months in social action, or been involved in a one-off activity lasting more than a day
- recognised that their activities had some benefit for both themselves and others.

According to their latest data, 39% of young people participated in meaningful social action in 2018 with those from the most affluent backgrounds more likely to have taken part in the past year (45% of ABC1 compared with 31% of C2DE). This is in line with a range of evidence that links participation to higher levels of education and social class. A lack of information (35%) or interest (31%) were reported as the most common barrier for not getting involved in social action, while socialising (23%) was the top reason for getting involved.

Although not a primary aim of the programme, the NCS aims for an overrepresentation of minority groups to help encourage greater social mobility. In 2017, 31% of their 99,179 participants came from BAME backgrounds. Their evaluation identified several positive outcomes three months on including the number of hours volunteered. However, there is a lack of information on longer term impact.

By age

In 2018/19, 65–74 year olds are the age group most likely to volunteer formally on a regular basis: More than one quarter (28%) volunteered at least once a month while more than a third (39%) volunteered at least once a year.

People aged 25–34 were least likely to formally volunteer compared to all other age groups. 15% volunteered at least once a month (regularly) and 29% at least once a year. This remains unchanged from previous years.

Participation levels among 16–24-year olds declined from the previous year (2017/18) – from 39% to 35% for volunteering at least once a year and from 24% to 21% for regular volunteering.

By gender

Women were more likely than men to have formally volunteered at least once in the last year (37% vs 34%) however levels of regular volunteering are similar (22% vs 21%).

Our Time Well Spent report highlights some gender differences in volunteering activities undertaken and causes supported. For example, women are less likely to be in representative volunteering roles, and men are more likely to be involved in sport and political organisations.

By employment status

Those in employment were more likely to formally volunteer on a regular basis than those who are unemployed (22% vs 17%), but those who are economically inactive were most likely to volunteer regularly (27%).

Our Time Well Spent data highlights that the majority of volunteers who are employed give time outside of work rather than through employer-supported volunteering.

By geography

In 2018/19, people living in rural areas were more likely to formally volunteer than those in urban areas (44% vs 34% at least once in the last year, and 29% vs 20% for regular volunteering).

In 2018/19 rates of formal volunteering were highest in the south-west, with 43% of people volunteering at least once in the last year and lowest in the West Midlands (29%).

By socio-economic status

In 2018/19, 14% were involved in formal volunteering regularly in the most deprived areas of England compared with 29% in the least deprived. There was less variation, however, for informal volunteering, especially for regular involvement.

These differences are confirmed by other research evidence, which also suggests that these differences are more significant for formal than informal volunteering.

The evidence also highlights that for formal volunteering, volunteers from lower socio-economic groups were less likely to undertake leading or organising roles, such as being a trustee.

2020

5 things councils should know about engaging young people, according to young people

By Ilona Lodewijckx

'Young people are the future.' When it comes to engaging and involving our youth, this quote is often mindlessly tossed about and hailed as a key motivator. Of course, empowering our youngest will serve us well for years to come, but young people are very much already here and ready to take part in the public debate. That's why we spoke with Emily and Justin, two inspiring young residents who are both actively involved in youth engagement programmes linked to North Ayrshire Council in Scotland.

Emily Nix (18) is a member of the Scottish Youth Parliament for Cunninghame South and the UK Youth Parliament for the West of Scotland. Justin Jones (16) is the Chairperson of the Irvine Youth Forum (a local body of youngsters representing the voice of young people at a local and national level). Both are also members and signatories of the North Ayrshire Youth Executive Committee, a group that regularly meets with the council. Justin and Emily have both actively been taking part in youth work programmes for several years. 'The first time I spoke at a cabinet meeting, I was only eleven years old,' says Emily.

Raising awareness on mental health, alleviating poverty in schools, offering information on drugs and addiction, explaining how a participatory budget works… the ongoing youth initiatives in North Ayrshire focus on an extensive range of topics. 'These issues are all interconnected,' says Justin. 'There's no way to treat diversity, poverty, and mental health as separate entities because they influence each other, and we can't tackle one without the other.'

Justin and Emily aren't just amplifying young voices in the local bodies and structures that allow it. They are actively involved in grass-root projects to improve the lives of young

Scots in the area. It's safe to say that many councils could learn from the leading example of the North Ayrshire council and its young residents, who get their hands dirty every day for the sake of their communities. That's why we asked Justin and Emily to share a few things councils should know about engaging the youth. After all, 'youngsters should be the first people to be consulted in matters that affect them, no matter how immature or uneducated they are.'

1. Engaging the youth means breaking a harmful tradition of exclusion

'Children must be seen, not heard.' Until not so long ago, this (outdated, terrible) phrase summarised the world's general perspective on young people's voices. Youth engagement is mostly a recent phenomenon, which councils are only now starting to embrace as a central part of their daily activities. Historically, young people have rarely—if ever—been consulted on the matters that affect them. And this, of course, has a significant impact on how they feel about participation to this day. 'If you know you won't be heard, what's the point of forming opinions?', wonders Emily. 'Young people might not be seeking information about topics close to their hearts, simply because they feel their opinions won't matter, anyway.'

It's often said that young people are generally harder to reach and engage in community engagement projects. This is often falsely attributed to a lack of interest or motivation. It's essential to realise that young people's non-participation is not an intrinsic characteristic, but something they've been taught. Even today, young people are still, sometimes unconsciously, discouraged to raise their voice. Because even though the times are gradually changing, youth engagement is still not where it's supposed to be. 'Even now, young people are often not taken seriously by those in decision-making roles. Too often, youth engagement is still tokenistic—they are engaging us for performative reasons, but not actually taking our voices into account. And that's just not right – we are constituents of the council, and they have the duty to listen to us,' says Emily.

Fortunately, if non-participation is not a problem inherent to young people, we can do something about it. By actively engaging and genuinely involving them in the matters that affect their lives, councils are ending a harmful tradition of exclusion and strengthening the democratic fabric of their communities.

2. Don't wait for young people to participate—bring participation to them

For the above-mentioned reason, councils shouldn't passively be waiting for young people to get involved. With the Joint Cabinet, the North Ayrshire Council, local members of the Scottish Youth Parliament, and the North Ayrshire Youth Executive Committee take matters into their own hands by visiting schools and organising conversation classes. Determined to let youngsters share ideas at their own pace, they lined the desks with paper tablecloth and asked them to jot down their ideas.

This kind of initiative doesn't only effectively enable youngsters to open up, it also shows a real effort and investment on the council's part. Meeting young people in their own environments and listening to what they have to say shows them your intentions are genuine.

Obviously, due to the COVID-19 pandemic, it's temporarily rather complicated to physically take your projects into schools or youth groups. But don't let social distancing deter you from trying. In North Ayrshire's first-ever digital Joint Cabinet, over 110 students took part in various discussions about the way the virus affects their 'community, digital connectivity, employability, and wellbeing'.

> **Youngsters should be the first people to be consulted in matters that affect them, no matter how immature or uneducated they are.**
>
> **Justin Jones**

3. Make participation as informal as possible

According to Justin and Emily, getting involved should also be fun. The tablecloth anecdote in the previous section is a good example of an initiative that is effective yet informal. It's really all about making participation as accessible as possible. 'One of the best things about youth work is that it continuously inspires people to join us. We care a lot about the different causes and learn a lot while campaigning, but some youngsters just get involved to have fun and make friends. And that's completely valid. We need to protect that informality, otherwise, we might scare people off. We are young, after all — we take youth work seriously, but that doesn't mean we have to be serious all the time,' says Emily.

If you're a council looking to engage local youth, this is an important thing to keep in mind. A copy-paste of previous participation projects or a one-size-fits-all approach simply won't suffice when targeting multiple or younger age groups. And instead of expecting youngsters to adjust to projects that weren't designed for them, think about what you as a council can do to tailor projects to their wants and needs. This might even help you inject a dose of fun into your general community engagement projects and lower the participation threshold for a more diverse range of adults as well.

> **You've got to realise you'll never stop building these relationships. You must instil that confidence in each individual young person who comes along.**
>
> **Emily Nix**

4. Young people will give it to you straight

Any age group or demographic can bring relevant insights to a community engagement project. After all, every group has particular experiences that shape their visions and opinions. Justin and Emily believe that young people's position at the boundary between child and adult gives them a unique perspective. 'As young people, we're bound to be in between. We're considered responsible enough for some things, too immature for others. It's a bizarre limbo, but it helps us see things in a different light,' says Emily.

Because of their age, young people tend to be less enmeshed with the existing state-of-affairs. According to Justin, this makes them less likely to sugar coat their input. 'Young people will tell it like it is,' says Justin. 'It's not about hurting feelings; it's about seeing what's wrong and putting it into words, and hopefully, into action.'

In short, engaging young people and gathering their opinions and ideas automatically injects your project with refreshing, relevant insights. And that, in turn, makes for policy-making that is not only more legitimate and supported but also simply more interesting and innovative.

5. Know this is a never-ending commitment

Much like Rome, successful youth engagement isn't built in a day. Or even two. 'These things take time,' says Justin. 'Empowering young people doesn't just happen overnight. Do as much as you can, slowly but surely, but know you probably won't be overwhelmed with responses the very first time you try something.' Engaging youth is a continuous effort that should lead to meaningful change. At its core, it's all about building trust: you can't expect young people to pour their hearts out if they've been told for decades their opinions don't matter. How do you build this trust? According to Justin, it's quite simple: 'make pledges, then deliver.'

Moreover, it's important to know that building this trust will be a long-term commitment. It's impossible to ever truly be 'done'. 'You've got to realise you'll never stop building these relationships. You must instil that confidence in each individual young person who comes along,' says Emily.

A gold mine of untapped potential

So, there you have it. Engaging local youth demands significant investment and a long-term commitment, but it's also fun, rewarding, and, to put it bluntly, a democratic non-negotiable. Young people are a gold mine of untapped potential to propel your community forward. Across Britain, thousands of youngsters like Justin and Emily have the drive to get their hands dirty for the betterment of their communities.

As for Justin and Emily, they'll keep doing what they're doing. Justin aims to continue being a voice for young people who are too shy to raise their own. Emily pledges to keep learning, because when it comes to youth activism, there's always something new on the horizon.

22 December 2020

Age is no limit to action

For the last ten months I have been school striking for the climate outside of my school every Friday morning. Why? Because I am afraid for my future.

By Holly Gillibrand

My name is Holly Gillibrand. I'm a 14-year-old environmentalist from Fort William.

That is something that no child should ever have to say, but in the 21st century my generation finds ourselves in a position where if we do not act now on the defining crisis of our time - climate and ecological breakdown - we may not have a future.

Scientists say that by the year 2030, climate breakdown will spiral out of control unless unprecedented changes in all aspects of our society have taken place. I will be 25-years-old, barely out of university and with my whole life ahead of me.

'Adults who disagree with the climate strikes often tell us that we should stay in school and get a good education. They then say that when we have become adults with the scientific knowledge required to solve this problem we can make the changes needed. There is only one problem in this otherwise flawless plan - when we have grown up, it will be too late. The climate crisis will already be irreversible.'

We are not just in a period of rapid climate breakdown, we are also in the midst of the sixth mass extinction. The extinction rate is 1,000 to 10,000 times faster than the background rate with up to 200 species going extinct every single day. According to the *Living Planet report*, 60% of life on Earth has been lost since 1970.

When I was younger, I had lots of dreams.

I wanted to be a vet, a zoologist, an actor. Now, I don't even know whether the planet is going to be habitable in the future and if my children will be able to experience what I and so many other generations have had the privilege of experiencing.

People often ask me what started my activism journey? I can tell you that it wasn't due to a sudden moment of realisation or awareness. It was the result of many, many years of being outside, climbing trees and building a connection with nature.

'My passion for the natural world and a raw, bitter frustration with the people in power culminated with me doing something that I never thought I would ever do in my life: I refused to go to school.'

When Greta Thunberg first sat down on school strike in front of the Swedish Parliament in August 2018, she had no idea that that small action of not going to school would kickstart the Fridays For Future movement. But it did and the school strike movement has grown so big in such a short period of time that on September 20th and 27th, over seven and a half million people went on strike for the climate. I think I can safely say that it is the biggest environmental movement in human history!

When I started striking in January, I didn't think that I could make a difference. I am after all just a small girl in a small town in the middle of the remote Scottish Highlands. I have since realised that I was wrong and Greta's quote, 'you are never too small to make a difference' continues to ring true.

In the past year I have spoken at numerous events and conferences. I am proud to be a young ambassador for Scotland: The Big Picture, a youth council member for Reserva: The Youth Land Trust and a volunteer for Scottish Youth Climate Strikes. I have taken my campaigning to Holyrood and Westminster, where I was privileged to meet Greta Thunberg, representatives from UK Student Climate Network and political party leaders including Caroline Lucas and Jeremy Corbyn.

I say these things - not to brag - but to show my age group that anyone can make a difference. We are the change we have been waiting for. And to all the young people reading this right now: get out there and change the world!

22nd November 2019

The power of Youth social action

An extract from the *#iwill campaign Impact Report.*

Why we need more young people to take action

A difficult time to be young

This is not an easy time to be growing up. More than a quarter of young people say they don't feel they belong in Britain[1]. Generation Z, the current generation of 10-20 year olds, are more likely to be depressed and less likely to interact with others in person.

They are facing: a society that is deeply divided; stalled social mobility[2]; significant uncertainties surrounding Brexit; a rapidly-changing labour market; technology that offers new threats as well as opportunities; and catastrophic changes to our climate unless urgent action is taken.

This is all happening against a backdrop of increased childhood poverty[3], a challenging funding environment for schools and colleges, and severe cuts to youth services in England[4].

Young people want to contribute

Despite all these challenges, young people want to improve their communities and make the world a better place. They have the power, energy, resourcefulness, passion and commitment to help address so many of the problems that society is facing.

Young people are already tackling 21st century challenges. Witness the Youth Strike 4 Climate that mobilised tens of thousands of school-age children across the UK this year. Young people are performing valuable services such as volunteering as hospital guides, befriending the chronically ill and acting as meal-time buddies. They're mentoring other young people and raising money for UK and overseas charities.

'Social action gives hope, it alleviates helplessness. It promotes community engagement and creates a consciousness which goes beyond personal goals.' – Dara McAnulty, 14, Castlewellan, NI

So why are we putting barriers in their way?

We know that young people have a great deal to contribute, so why do we make it so hard for them to do that? Too often, organisations shy away from working with young people. Even in the voluntary sector, young people are not being included in the decision-making process. According to the Charities Aid Foundation, 18-24 year olds account for less than 0.5% of all charity trustees, despite making up 12% of Britain's population[5].

We all need to step up to make it easier for young people to contribute to our society.

'Young people are often disregarded as "snowflakes" who are said to be prone to taking more offence and having less psychological resilience than generations before us. But I believe that it is the young people of today that are changing the world, by becoming more aware of critical issues that must be solved.' – Anna McGovern, 17, Kent

Many ways to make a difference

The #iwill campaign defines 'youth social action' as activities that young people do that make a positive difference to others or to the environment. It can encompass many different things, from starting a school petition or picking up litter in a local park, to visiting people in a care home or campaigning for action on climate change.

Whether they're participating in a local activity or working for a global movement, young people across the country are taking action to create a better society.

'If we don't do something, who will? Hoping for change isn't enough, we have to create change and implement hope.' – Lucy Aur Keeling, 19, Llanelli

High quality social action benefits us all

When young people take part in high quality social action, everyone benefits:

♦ Organisations benefit from young people's energy, ideas and capacity to create positive change. They gain a different perspective that can shift their way of thinking and open up new ways of working.

♦ Communities benefit when young people feel valued, engaged and involved. It can create a greater sense of community and boost social cohesion and integration[6].

- Young people develop their character and confidence. They experience higher levels of wellbeing that can help improve their mental resilience. They also develop vital skills and networks that can support future employment[7].

'Social action gives me so much more confidence and pride. It makes you realise how privileged you are, and how you can change other people's lives.'– Ella Kiely, 12, Twickenham

What does great youth social action look like?

Research by the Institute for Voluntary Research and the Young Foundation suggests that high quality activities will meet **six principles**. They will:

1. be youth-led

2. be challenging

3. have social impact

4. allow progress into other opportunities

5. be embedded in a young person's life

6. enable reflection about the value of the activity

Creating a habit for life

Starting a journey of social action at a young age is critical. The Habits of Service research by the Jubilee Centre for Character and Virtues[8] demonstrated the value of starting early and exposing young people to meaningful opportunities to make a positive contribution.

> The research found that those who first get involved in service under the age of 10 are:
>
> **2x More than twice as likely to form a habit of service than if they start aged 16–18 years.**
>
> **More likely to be involved in a wider range of service activities and to participate in them more frequently.**
>
> **More likely to identify themselves more closely with moral and civic values such as open-mindedness, compassion and hope.**

'My social action has given me a direction for the career I plan to follow later in life and taught me about resilience, enthusiasm and the difference we can make even as young people.'– Lily Macfarlane, 15, Cambridge

What young people are telling us

The National Youth Social Action survey was established in 2014 to measure the extent to which 10-20 year olds are taking part in social action in the UK.

The survey, commissioned by DCMS and conducted by Ipsos Mori on behalf of the #iwill campaign, asks over 2,000 young people across the UK each year to share how and why they get involved in social action if they do, or reasons for not taking part if they don't.

For the purposes of the survey, we say that young people have taken part in 'meaningful social action' if they have:

- Been involved in social action in the past 12 months.

- Participated in social action at least every few months or taken part in a one-off activity lasting more than a day in the last 12 months.

- Recognised a benefit to themselves and others and/or the environment because of their social action.

Young people are taking action in many different ways

According to our survey, young people say they have **most frequently**:

- Participated in a fund raising or sponsored event (43%)

- Given time to help a charity or cause (26%)

- Supported other people who aren't friends or relatives (23%)

Young people are **less likely** to say they have:

- Campaigned for something they believe in (8%)

- Been involved in youth advisors' groups (6%)

Sustained activity, for example over the course of a few months or more, was more common among those who are campaigning for something they believe in.

Young people want to help

Just 5% of adults think that young people today are very likely to take part in social action[9]. Survey responses show that this perception must be urgently challenged and changed. The vast majority of young people are eager to make a difference in society and want to make the world a better place:

> **81% Care about contributing to make the world a better place for everyone**
>
> **82% Believe they have things they can offer to others**
>
> **74% Believe they make a difference in the world**

Young people who have taken part in meaningful social action were much more likely to believe they could have a positive impact than those who had rarely or never taken part in social action over the last 12 months. Perhaps unsurprisingly, those from wealthier backgrounds also had more confidence in their ability to make a positive impact than their less affluent peers.

Who's taking part?

In the past 12 months, 6 out of 10 young people have taken part in activities to help others and/or the environment. However, only 4 out of 10 have taken part in meaningful social action. Both of these figures are consistent with participation rates in previous years.

6 out of 10 young people have taken part in activities to help others and/or the environment

4 out of 10 have taken part in meaningful social action

A stark participation gap is evident. Young people from lower-income backgrounds are significantly less likely to have taken part in meaningful social action than their wealthier peers: 27% of young people from social class group DE compared to 52% in group AB.

Girls remain more likely than boys to participate, although the gap is small (40% for girls, compared with 37% for boys).

The survey also found that young people who have taken part in meaningful social action were more committed to making a difference to others and/or the environment in the future.

Notes:

1. National Citizen Service (2017), https://inews.co.uk/news/ education/ quarter-young-people-feel-not-belong-britain/
2. Social Mobility Commission (2019), State of the Nation in 2018-19: Social Mobility in Great Britain, https://assets. publishing.service.gov.uk/ Government/uploads/system/ uploads/attachment_data/file/798404/ SMC_State_of_the_ Nation_Report_2018-19.pdf
3. Child Poverty Action Group (2018), www.cpag.org.uk/ content/uk-child-poverty-gaps-increasing-again
4. www.bbc.co.uk/news/education-43668167
5. Charities Aid Foundation, (2015), Young Trustees Guide, https://www.cafonline.org/docs/default-source/about-us- publications/ youngtrusteesreport_1682a_web_080915.pdf
6. Demos (2015), Service Nation 2020 https://dera.ioe. ac.uk/24131/1/ ServiceNation2020.pdf
7. Behavioural Insights Team (2016), Evaluating Social Action, https://www. bi.team/publications/evaluating- youth-social-action-final-report/
8. Jubilee Centre for Character and Virtues, University of Birmingham, (2017), Habit of Service, https://www. jubileecentre.ac.uk/1581/projects/ current-projects/a- habit-of-service
9. Royal Society of the Arts (2018), Teenagency: How Young People Are Changing the World, https://www.thersa.org/ discover/publications-and-articles/reports/teenagency- how-young-people-can-create-a-better-world

May 2019

Likelihood to engage in social action activities in next 12 months

Already engaged in meaningful social action (93%)

All young people (60%)

% of young people that take part in meaningful social action

Low income background (27%)

Wealthiest background (52%)

Three in five young people (60%) say they are 'likely' to engage in social action activities, compared with 93% of those who have been involved with meaningful social action.

Half of those who have taken part in meaningful social action were more likely to say they 'definitely will' take part in the next 12 months (49%), compared with 25% of young people overall.

Teen discovers passion for volunteering

Ashur Cali, 16, from Leeds has a whole new outlook on volunteering and a more positive outlook on life after completing the National Citizen Service's (NCS) 'Keep Doing Good' programme.

Had 2020 gone to plan, Ashur, was due to go away on the traditional NCS programme this summer to live independently, meet new people, develop new skills and contribute to making a difference in the community. However, social distance restrictions meant this was not possible, Ashur was still able to make a difference in the community through completing NCS's' Keep Doing Good' programme. 'Keep Doing Good' aims to pledge 1 million volunteering hours into local communities to help them bounce back from the impact of COVID-19.

Before the two week 'Keep Doing Good' programme, Ashur thought that volunteering was limited to working for free for a company and wasn't aware of the charity work he was able to get involved with. Whilst on 'Keep Doing Good' Ashur took part in some volunteering at Shine community garden in Leeds. The gardens provide the local community with a scenic place escape to, relax and enjoy a little bit of countryside in the heart of the city. After helping with the renovating of the gardens, Ashur has a much better understanding of volunteering and is keen to volunteer again the future. He would also like others to be inspired by what the group have done, and get involved with volunteering themselves.

Ashur said:

'I've not only volunteered and done some good but I now feel a lot better than I did before starting the program. My time has been spent doing something worthwhile and bringing something positive to another person's day.

Whilst on 'Keep Doing Good' Ashur developed his teamwork skills. The group was tasked with gathering and debating ideas for a Social Action Project before presenting them as a group.

Ashur said:

'At the start of the two weeks, I would have put myself forward for a leadership role, leading and making decisions, assuming I was the best at the job. However, the time with NCS has taught me the value of stepping back and listening to others and that not only my voice matters in a collaborative environment. Now, I loosen the reins in a way and allow other members of the team to make a choice and I will follow their leadership, more of a team player than before the program.'

Stacey Fannan, Team Leader at Learn By Design, noticed a change in Ashur and said:

'On day one Ashur was a quietly confident young person. Always keen to give an answer or volunteer to take charge. He has been a driving force amongst the team from the get-go. However, a noticeable change in Ashur is although he is confident and first to offer an answer or response, he would doubt himself in his answer especially if challenged. Now on the final day, Ashur is quick to answer and able to confidently give justification for his answers and positively meet challenges. He also made positive development in his teamwork and listening skills and can work collaboratively to achieve team goals.'

9 September 2020

How youth volunteering increases young voter turnout: the impact on citizenship

By Dr Stuart Fox

The central finding of *Social Action as a Route to the Ballot Box*: youth volunteering increases turnout among young people by increasing their interest in political issues and so raising their motivation to vote. This effect is only apparent, however, for young people whose parents have little or no interest in politics (and who are unlikely to socialise their children into being politically active).

Those from more politically engaged households are considerably more likely to volunteer but are also already likely to be interested in politics, and so receive less of a benefit from their volunteering. The impact of volunteering on young people's political interest is only part of the story, however. This project has also considered how volunteering affects young people's views of their duty to vote in elections.

Previous research has argued (but never effectively demonstrated) that young people who volunteer are likely to develop more of an attachment to their local community and as a result feel more of an obligation to be active in community affairs. Alternatively, others have argued that as volunteering brings young people into contact with social problems (such as pollution or homelessness) and people in need, they become more likely to feel they have a duty to participate in politics to try and address those issues. Either way, it is expected that young people who volunteer become more likely to vote as a result of seeing it as their civic duty.

This project shows that the previous research is partially correct: young people who volunteer are more likely to believe they have a duty to vote in elections when they are older. As with political interest, however, this consequence of volunteering is primarily felt by those raised by parents who do not see voting as a civic duty and so are unlikely to socialise their children into holding such a view. Fig. 1 (see below) illustrates this, using data from a sub-sample of young people in the *UK Household Longitudinal Study (UKHLS)* aged between 15 and 22 (and who had never voted before) around the 2015 UK General Election.[1]

Fig. 1 compares the political interest of the young people in the 2011/13 *UKHLS* survey with their belief that voting is a civic duty around the 2015 election in the 2014/16 survey (questions about voting as a civic duty were not asked to most of the respondents in the earlier survey). While there is not a perfect correlation between being interested in politics and seeing voting as a duty, the two are related, and we expect those who are interested in politics during childhood to be more likely to see voting as a duty when they are older.

What is of interest to this research is whether those who volunteered between the 2011/13 and 2014/16 surveys were more likely than those who did not to see voting as a civic duty, which would suggest a 'volunteer effect'. The graph also accounts for the impact of the attitudes towards voting the respondents were likely to be exposed to at home, by categorising them depending on the beliefs of their parents regarding the civic duty of voting.

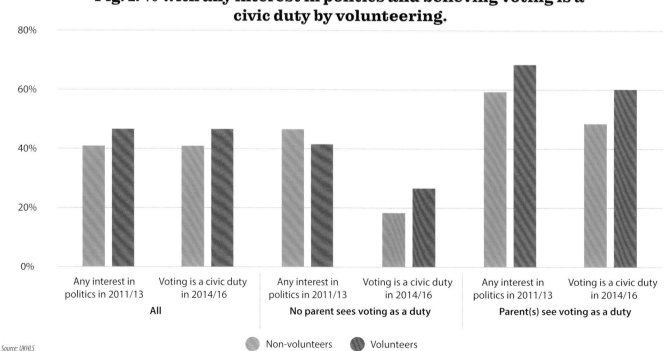

Fig. 1: % with any interest in politics and believing voting is a civic duty by volunteering.

Source: UKHLS

Looking at the whole sample reveals no evidence of a substantial 'volunteer effect': 41 per cent of non-volunteers were interested in politics in 2011/13, and the same proportion saw voting as a duty in 2014/16; among volunteers, the figures were 47 and 48 per cent respectively.

A larger difference is apparent, however, when respondents are categorised based on their parents' view of voting as a duty. For respondents whose parents saw voting as a duty, 60 per cent of non-volunteers were interested in politics in 2011/13 and 49 per cent saw voting as a duty in 2014/16; for volunteers, the figures were 69 and 60 per cent respectively. In other words, more young people who volunteered were likely to see voting as a duty when they were older than those who did not volunteer, even though overall a sizeable minority rejected the notion of having a civic obligation to vote.

Among respondents whose parents did not see voting as a duty, the volunteer effect was even larger: for non-volunteers, the proportion who saw voting as a duty in 2014/16 was 29-points smaller than that who were interested in politics in 2011/13, while for volunteers this drop was just 15-points.

Schemes that promote youth volunteering, therefore, can be effective means of helping more young people to vote in elections – particularly those from politically disengaged households. They not only increase young people's motivation to vote, but their perceived civic obligation to do so as well. If such schemes can be organised so as to recruit more young people from disengaged households (something they are currently not particularly successful in doing, as future blog posts will highlight), they could be very effective in helping to reduce age inequalities in turnout.

Notes: 1 The main analyses for this project were conducted using a range of complex statistical methods, including logistic regression analysis, latent structure analysis and structural equation modelling. An illustrative summary of the key findings are presented here and in future blog posts – more details of the methods or findings are available upon request.

The sample for this data included 2,063 respondents who were not yet eligible to vote, or became eligible to vote in their first General Election in 2015, in the 2014/16 UKHLS survey, and who provided complete data for the required variables in the UKHLS Youth Panel in 2011/13 and 2012/14, and the main panel in 2014/16. All were aged between 15 and 22 in the final survey. The data on volunteering was collected in the 2012/14 Youth Panel survey. With the data on parents' civic duty included – which was collected from respondents' parents in the 2011/13 Main Panel, the sample size fell to 602.

6 June 2019

For young people, a 'moral' choice?

By Helen Haste, Emeritus Professor in the Department of Psychology at the University of Bath

The media are predicting a 'youthquake' in the coming election. This may be hyperbole (or hope) but there are signs that young people are taking it seriously. The largest proportion of recent registrations to vote have come from young people – though one in three have still not registered. What does this mean?

Youth participation in national elections fluctuates but always seems to make news - whether because of 'apathy' or the opposite. The Obama election in 2008 was seen as a beacon of positive youth commitment – and a triumph for social media use – but other elections in the world did not always match up. Do people worry that a whole generation will never vote, or do we assume that they will grow into their civic duty in due course? Is lack of electoral interest in young people an indictment of youth's irresponsibility, or of the system that fails to inspire the public in general?

We do know some things about youth civic participation. In particular, we know that party affiliation is not a strong factor. Several international studies show that 'joining a political party' comes last or very far down the list of important characteristics of being a 'good citizen'. Young people become actively involved in civic issues usually for one of two reasons. One, they become attached to a group primarily for social reasons, but become drawn into the issues or cause through their friends. Two, they become morally engaged on a single issue. Because they come to care about the issue, they feel a strong motivation to support action, or to take action themselves. This may be confined to that one issue, or it may widen interest and awareness as the context of the issue, and policies or structures underlying it, become apparent. So a specific event, or example, may eventually lead to wider commitment to a broader social movement.

However this may still not be about party affiliation. Many recent issues that have fired young people are not exclusively tied to one party – though political parties may try to capitalise on hot current issues. The environment, climate change, feminism, gender and ethnic politics, all seem to have a broadly 'liberal' (in the US sense) perspective, but this is in part because there are some vociferous 'conservative' (with a small 'c') counter narratives. There are plenty of at least centre right environmentalists and people concerned about gender and racial equality – even if their 'solutions' might differ a little from the Left. I am fascinated by the history of the very rapid progress of the environment movement. Forty years ago 'eco-warriors' were definitely on the political fringe. Yet remarkably soon primary school children were engaged with saving the rainforest animals, and urging their parents to buy eco food. The environment is mainstream, recycling is morally and legally mandatory, and – with a little help in the UK from national treasure Sir David Attenborough – there is rapidly mounting pressure to take climate change more seriously.

So what will young people latch on to on December 12, and how will it affect the parties? We know that, first, young people are more likely to vote Labour than Conservative, and to be Remainers rather than Brexiteers. Recent polls show that fewer than 25% of under-35s will vote Conservative, compared to around 60% of their grandparents. Around three quarters of young people voted to Remain in 2016. (I sometimes wonder what might have happened if 250,000 of them had not been corralled at Glastonbury on the voting day…).

If Brexit – as seems to be the case – is the dominant 'motivating single issue' of the election, how might young people respond? First, will they choose to support whichever local party candidate endorses their view on Brexit? Or will they specifically vote against the local candidate whose party opposes their view? The first option would be voting consistent with one's beliefs. The second is tactical – it might involve voting for a party not wholly aligned with one's core beliefs. Do we expect young people to vote tactically? In our 'first past the post' system, tactical voting makes sense (I have only twice in my life voted for the Party closest to my beliefs, because in the constituencies in which I have lived, it would be a wasted vote; so I vote to oppose the Party I do not wish to see in power).

Many young people may be inclined to vote Green, but in almost all constituencies this would be a 'wasted' vote and have no 'Brexit impact' – either way. For Remainers, in constituencies with a strong Lib Dem candidate, the choice is clear-cut. Otherwise it is not. By no means all Tory candidates are Brexiteers. Labour's position is also ambiguous. It will be interesting to see how young people make sense of this and play it out.

2 December 2019

UK volunteering soars during coronavirus crisis

Ten million have helped in their community – most plan to continue after lockdown ends.

By Rupert Jones

Ten million UK adults have been volunteering in their community during the coronavirus crisis, and most say they will carry on after the lockdown ends, according to new research.

The study also found that Britons have been extending a financial helping hand to local businesses. More than £1 billion was spent on services and goods that people knew they would never be able to use during the pandemic, including payments to home cleaners and gardeners.

Since the crisis took hold, millions of Britons have been serving as an informal 'volunteering army', whether it is helping with grocery shopping for others, picking up prescriptions, ringing up people living alone, or helping out at a local food bank.

According to the research from insurer Legal & General and the Centre for Economics and Business Research, one in five UK adults (19%) has volunteered their time for community activities since the start of the lockdown on 23 March.

With each individual contributing, on average, about three hours of their time, the work this volunteer army is doing is estimated to have an equivalent economic value of more than £350 million a week.

The researchers said 'Britain's community spirit has doubled down in lockdown' and that these volunteers were a key part of the 'national infrastructure' during the crisis.

Nigel Wilson, Legal & General's chief executive, said: 'We have become a nation of volunteers during the Covid-19 crisis. And – judging by the millions who plan to continue after the lockdown – it is a change that is here to stay.'

Two-thirds of those who have volunteered (67%) have been doing grocery shopping for neighbours, friends and others, while a quarter (26%) have collected and delivered medicines or prescriptions. Meanwhile, 16% of those donating their time have volunteered to phone people who may be struggling with loneliness or other issues. This is all on top of the help being provided via the NHS volunteer programme launched on 24 March.

The research found that millennials – typically defined as those born between the early 1980s and the late 1990s or the start of the 2000s – were the least likely age group to volunteer, but that when they did, they gave up the most time: an average of 3.5 hours a week on grocery shopping, and 4.4 hours if volunteering in other ways.

Meanwhile, across all those surveyed, more than three-quarters (78%) said they planned to continue helping those in need after the lockdown.

The researchers also found that many households had tried to help those who help them, and were continuing to pay cleaners, gardeners and other workers for services they knew they would never be able to use under lockdown. An estimated £637 million was spent on unused goods and services between the start of the lockdown and the end of April – a figure that has now risen to more than £1 billion.

26 May 2020

Virtues, volunteering and Coronavirus

By Claire Jackson

These are very strange times that we are living in – as I'm sure you have already noticed. It's easy to feel overcome with anxiety and helplessness at the current situation the coronavirus outbreak has caused. However, there are things that we can all do to help one another, and, through doing so, help ourselves. Amidst the severity of the daily updates on the spread of the virus, the world's media has also been highlighting virtuous behaviours displayed by individuals and groups, such as volunteering, service, and 'acts of kindness'.

Benefits of volunteering

Here at the Jubilee Centre, we have explored the 'double benefit' that many gain from volunteering, whereby through helping others, we both benefit society and ourselves through character development and increased wellbeing. Studies, such as that by Pine et al. (2018), have found that volunteering to support those affected by a disaster or crisis can potentially help to reduce the volunteers' stress and anxiety induced by the event(s). Dr Yvonne Su, who researches people's responses to disasters, has found that 'community humanitarian responses' tend to emerge quickly; 'generally… smaller acts of altruism and solidarity that help to make those helping and those being helped feel better and stronger in the face of a crisis'.

There are already many incredible groups and individuals supporting their communities to get through the crisis. Worldwide acts of kindness are being regularly reported on by news outlets, as well as those more locally. From the Jubilee Centre's perspective, it is particularly interesting to see which virtues and character strengths are the media championing through these accounts. What sort of people are we being told to emulate? And, given this is very much a global crisis, does this profile change in different parts of the world?

Virtuous behaviours around the world

Unsurprisingly, civic virtues such as volunteering, neighbourliness and community awareness resonate throughout the reports. In Canada, the concept of 'caremongering' has taken root, coined by a group of people who wanted to flip the narrative of 'scaremongering' and support vulnerable people in their communities. In China, where volunteer call-handlers have proven crucial, individuals such as Liu Xiaofeng have received recognition. Liu started her volunteering service in 1976 as a secondary school student in response to another crisis, the Tangshang earthquake. From then 'the habit stuck', and although Liu had resigned from volunteering four years ago, she stepped back up to support people through this new crisis. Liu appears to be a shining example of an individual with a 'habit of service'. (She also demonstrates humility in her assertion that she is 'just an ordinary woman'!).

There are some subtle differences in the virtues both explicitly and implicitly championed across the world's media. In Italy, which has been hit especially hard by the virus, key figures such as the Pope encourage people to continue to keep their hope and faith, two of the three core theological virtues of the Catholic Church. Giuseppe Conte, the Italian Prime Minister, has praised the courage and determination of his nation.

India has also begun to adopt the Canadian 'caremongering' initiative, thanks to the work of Mahita Nagaraj, who learned about it through the media. Increasingly threatened by an outbreak of coronavirus, Indian media has focused on the generosity of different groups and individuals, and gratitude towards those offering help. Informal volunteers in Spain are acting out of respect for their elderly neighbours, and have adopted a new unofficial anthem of resilience, a 1990s Spanish hit song titled Resistire. In addition to 'caremongering', Canadians have focused on social justice and tolerance, as well as displaying love to others.

And, of course, there are the 750,000 people who responded to the call for NHS Volunteer Responders here in the UK, far surpassing the original target of 250,000 sign-ups. The Royal Voluntary Service, responsible for the volunteer drive, has also written about Britain's age-old commitment to volunteering in crises.

Which virtues are being celebrated?

Hence, the virtues that the media have chosen to highlight in the efforts of 'ordinary' people are largely civic (volunteering, neighbourliness, community awareness, service) and moral (love, kindness, gratitude, respect, tolerance). There are also several references to the need for performance virtues such as resilience, determination and courage, but few regarding intellectual virtues (apart from occasionally creativity).

Going forward, it is heartening to read stories of these virtuous behaviours and individuals across the world, especially when experiences of empty shelves and using the threat of coronavirus as a 'weapon' are also prevalent. As the NCVO reminds us that we are facing 'a marathon, not a sprint' in our volunteering efforts, perhaps this crisis (and the extra time many of us now have!) offers us an opportunity to hone and habituate these character strengths our communities increasingly need from us.

2 April 2020

Why are we altruistic?

There is more into doing good than you might think. Whether it's from a philanthropic spark of the moment that you decide to donate to a local charity, or from volunteering for those less fortunate, the truth is that the undercurrent of altruism has been running through you since birth.

When does it start?

Altruism, a foundation for doing good, is the motivational intent of increasing the welfare of others, even if it can be at the consequence of your own. According to a study by Megan M. Filkowski, Ph.D. and others, signs of altruistic intent have been noted in infants as young as 14-18 months through behaviours such as helping other infants grasp out-of-reach objects or opening cabinet doors, with no adult encouragement or supervision. Other minor acts of kindness fall under the scale of altruism, such as offering your seat to an elderly individual on the bus or holding the door open for others – acts which hold no particular benefit or reward to you. Despite this lack of reward or clear incentive, there lies a reason behind altruistic, pro-social action and its unsolicited appearance in youth.

Chemically speaking

Among sixty chemical elements or so in our body, one stands out for altruism. Dopamine is an organic chemical synthesized in the brain and kidneys, and is often associated with a sensation of reward and satisfaction. While these feelings are often elicited through base motivations such as fulfilling food cravings and other forms of gratification, research has found that the very act of doing good for others is capable of evoking dopamine. In a study by William T. Harbaugh, Ph.D. and others, volunteers were placed in an fMRI while tasked with playing the 'dictator game' – a test in which participants will be given a sum of money, and in certain stages be tasked with either voluntarily or mandatorily donating money to a food bank. Any money they reserve will be theirs to keep. Harbaugh found that during these donation stages, parts of the nucleus accumbens – a part of the brain responsible for emotions including sensations of reward – would activate. Those who would voluntarily donate a larger sum of money – 'entitled altruists' – than those who donated little to none – 'entitled egoists', saw significantly greater activity within the nucleus accumbens. This activity indicated a greater rush of satisfaction and in turn, dopamine. Those who experienced greater activity would go on to donate more throughout the entire experiment in response to this sensation.

Cell longevity

There is, however, more to altruism than the sensation of satisfaction. Within a journal published by Stephen G. Post, Ph.D. lies a multitude of accumulated studies and research which correlates stress and altruism to longevity. Post found over a collection of studies that the beneficial sensations evoked by altruism are able to overpower other sensations, such as fear, depression, hate, and anxiety. The benefits that altruism poses offset a number of emotions that cause stress that, if long-lasting, can shorten telomere length. Telomeres are protective caps at the ends of chromosomes that prevent DNA deterioration, thereby acting to extend cell longevity.

Stress also adversely impacts the immune and cardiovascular systems, resulting in greater degradation. Through the positive effects of doing good, one can altogether distract the body from the harmful stress associated with age or other detrimental factors and experience a happier, longer, and more fulfilling life.

The loop

This poses the question: is there such a thing as pure, unselfish altruism where there is no personal good gained from voluntary good deeds? The short answer is no, yet the selfishness of altruism is one that ought to be celebrated and put into practice. By effectively practising altruism for the purpose of helping others, you will inadvertently be doing good unto yourself, both extending and enriching your own life. With less stress, greater amounts of dopamine, and a healthier life, you will be able to continue to fuel your motivation for altruistic good deeds and in turn, be able to continue helping others. The happiness you feel when doing good will result in greater happiness, which will entice you to do more good. What results is a classic feedback loop of consistently doing good for those in need.

Armed with this knowledge, you have all the reasons you need to get out there and do good. Embrace the altruist within you, and not only will you be granting others a better life in ways big or small, but you will also be bettering your own life, too.

The morality of feeling equal empathy for strangers and family alike

THE CONVERSATION

An article from *The Conversation*.

By Brendan Gaesser, Assistant Professor of Psychology, University at Albany, State University of New York and Zoë Fowler, Graduate Assistant, University at Albany, State University of New York

The year 2020 has been no stranger to suffering. In the midst of a global pandemic, widespread financial hardship and violence arising from systemic racism, empathy for others' suffering has been pushed to the front and centre in U.S. society.

As society grapples to find its moral compass in a time of such hardship and strife, a critical question emerges: Whose suffering should one care about?

When you ponder who is worth feeling empathy for, friends, family members and children might come to mind. But what about strangers, or people not connected to you through nationality, social status or race?

As cognitive scientists, we wanted to understand what moral beliefs people hold about empathy and how these beliefs may shift depending on whom someone is feeling empathy for.

Empathy as a force for good

Evidence suggests that empathy – broadly defined as the ability to understand and share in someone else's experience – can be a force for good. Numerous studies have shown it often leads to altruistic helping behaviour.

Further, feeling empathy for a member of a stigmatized group can reduce prejudice and improve attitudes toward the entire stigmatized group.

But there has also been research suggesting empathy may contribute to bias and injustice. Studies have shown that people tend to feel more empathy for the suffering of those who are close and similar to themselves, such as someone of the same race or nationality, than for those who are more distant or dissimilar. This bias in empathy has consequences. For example, people are less likely to donate time or money to help someone of a different nationality compared with someone of their own nationality.

Neuroscientists have shown that this bias is evident in how our brains process both firsthand and secondhand pain. In one such study, participants received a painful shock and also watched another person receive a painful shock. There was greater similarity in participants' neural activity when the person they observed rooted for the same sports team as themselves.

Whether empathy has a positive impact on society or not has been the subject of a fierce debate spanning politics, philosophy and psychology. Some scholars have suggested

empathy should be denounced as too narrow in scope and inherently biased to have a place in our moral lives.

Others have argued that empathy is a particularly potent force that can motivate many people to help others and can be expanded to be more inclusive.

What is largely left unconsidered is whether it could actually be our sense of what is right and wrong that limits our empathy. Perhaps many of us believe that inequality in empathy is right – that we should care more for those who are close and similar to us. In other words, loyalty is a greater moral force than equality.

The morality of empathy

In 2020, we ran a study to better understand the morality of empathy.

Three hundred participants from across the U.S. completed a study in which they were presented with a story describing an individual who is learning about global food scarcity. The individual reads about the struggles of two people in the story, one who is socially close – a friend or a family member – and another who is socially distant: for example, from a distant country. In different versions, the person in the story is described as feeling empathy for the stranger or for the friend or family member, or for both people equally, or for neither.

After reading the story, participants then rated how morally right or wrong they thought it was for this person to feel empathy in this manner.

When presented with stories in which the person feels either empathy solely for the friend/family member or the socially distant person, participants typically respond that it is more moral to feel empathy for the friend/family member. But participants judged feeling equal empathy as the most moral. Equal empathy was rated as 32% more morally right than feeling empathy for just one person in the story.

Friend or stranger?

Although this study suggested that people believed it more moral to have equal empathy, it left certain questions

unanswered: What was behind the perceived morality of equal empathy? And would this pattern hold if people were judging their own feelings on empathy?

So we ran a follow-up study with a new sample of 300 people. This time we changed the story so that it was from the participants' own perspective, and the two people in need were people they personally knew – one being someone close to them, the other an acquaintance. We also added endings to the story, so that participants could now also feel empathy for both people but to different degrees.

The results were remarkably similar to the first study: Feeling more empathy for one's close friend or family member was seen as more moral. But most notably, feeling equal empathy for both people was again judged as the most moral outcome.

Where to go from here?

In a moment when fostering a culture of caring for those who are different seems challenging, our research may offer some insight and perhaps hope. It suggests that most people believe we should care about everyone equally.

With the right approach, this belief in the morality of equal empathy may even translate to real changes. Recent work has shown that empathy can be increased based on one's motivation and personal beliefs. For example, participants who wrote a letter about how empathy can be grown and developed showed improvements in their ability to recognize others' emotions, a major part of empathy.

We are undoubtedly living through an age in which people are divided by race, nationality and political affiliation. But we are all human beings, and we all deserve to be cared for on some level. Our research provides evidence that this principle of equality in empathy is not some obscure ideal. Rather, it is a tenet of our moral beliefs.

22 December 2020

Young people have the biggest gender gap in blood donation

Women aged 17-34 are almost twice as likely to donate than men the same age.

◆ Women aged 17-34 are almost twice as likely to donate than men the same age, exposing the real need for more young men to donate blood

◆ The busy lifestyles of 17-34-year-olds could be putting some off donating, with one in six saying they know it's a good thing to do but haven't got around to it

◆ To tackle this gender gap and recruit more young blood donors, NHS Blood and Transplant is launching a two-week national campaign with ITV2

Young men are being urged to get involved in blood donation in a campaign launched on 17 October 2019 by NHS Blood and Transplant (NHSBT) and ITV2, as new figures reveal women aged 17-34 are almost twice as likely to donate than men the same age (1). This is despite the need for men's blood because it can more easily be used to stop bleeding from surgery or injuries.

The latest blood donation figures show young people have the biggest gender gap in blood donation. In the last year, 172,600 blood donors were young women (17-34-year olds), compared with 105,900 men the same age, and amongst this age group two thirds of new registrations were women (2), highlighting the important need for more young men to register to donate blood and save lives.

It is important that young men continuously register as blood donors because as people get older they're less likely to be able to donate (3). Men are particularly important

donors, as they make up most long-term blood donors. They are more likely to have lots of iron, so can donate more regularly than women.

Men's blood can also be more easily used for platelets, which are used to treat people in emergencies when they are bleeding a lot. Conversely, women often have breaks in donation due to pregnancy.

It is not fully understood why fewer young men donate than women, but previous research by NHSBT found that one in five (20%) men in general admit they fear needles and one in four (24%) fear giving blood (4).

The busy lifestyles and frequent travel of many young people could be putting some off donating blood. Amongst 17-34-year-old men and women, one in six (17%) have said they know it's a good thing to do but haven't got around to it (5).

Mike Stredder, Director of Blood Donation at NHS Blood and Transplant, says: 'We need 400 people to register as new donors every day to maintain the blood supply, for the best chance of keeping patients alive.

'For many reasons it's vital that young people continue to register and donate – particularly young men – not least because older people become less likely to be able to donate blood. Please do something amazing and book an appointment to start saving lives, especially if you live or work near to one of our donor centres.'

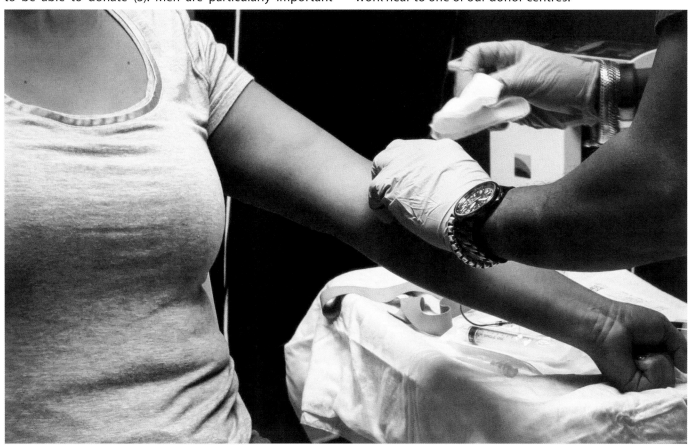

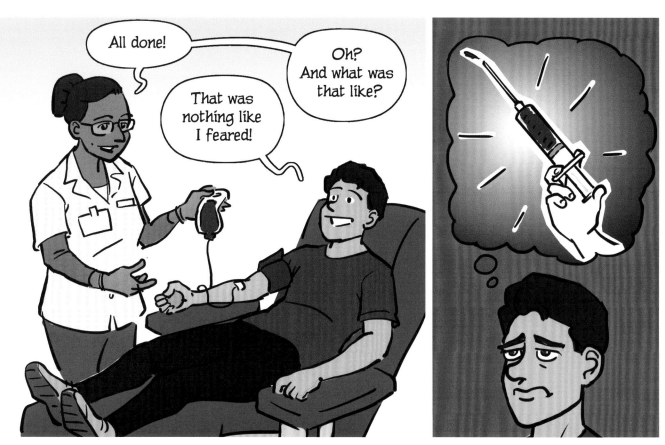

Despite this, overall, young people are showing a huge commitment to their environment, giving blood in their hundreds of thousands. Last year 17-34-year-olds supplied 450,000 whole blood donations of a total 1.48 million, making up almost a third of donations (6).

For the second year running NHSBT and ITV2 have partnered to inspire young people to register and donate blood, so they can continue to play their important role in blood donation.

Clare Phillips, ITV Director of Social Purpose, says: 'ITV has the ability to shape culture for good and the ITV2 Blood Squad campaign is a great example of how TV can change behaviour and make a real impact.

'We were thrilled with the success of the ITV2 Blood Squad last year, 33,000 sign ups were made to the blood donor register with the potential to improve and save up to 100,000 lives.

'We have even bigger ambitions for this campaign in 2019. It will be one of the ways that ITV will meet its target of encouraging 10 million people to take action to improve their physical or mental health by 2023.'

Adverts, featuring popular TV personalities from ITV2's shows, will run from 17 October for two weeks on ITV2, online, on radio, in cinema and across social media to emphasise that there's no need to fear blood donation this Halloween.

During the campaign month last year thousands of people were inspired to register and their donations have saved or improved the lives of up to 30,000 people – it is hoped this year's campaign will achieve the same and more.

♦ The appeal is targeted at people living near the 23 permanent donor centres because the donor centres have more capacity for new donors.

♦ To register to give blood, visit blood.co.uk or download the GiveBlood app.

♦ Find a future appointment – most new donors give blood within three months of registering.

Notes to editors

1. Figures recorded by NHSBT show there were 825,340 active whole blood donors between 1 September 2018 and 31 august 2019 – of which 278,591 were aged 17-34. Amongst 17-34-year-old donors, 172,661 were women and 105,930 were men. Analysis of this data shows women aged 17-34 are 63% (X1.6) more likely to donate compared to men the same age.

2. Figures recorded by NHSBT show between 1 September 2018 and 31 August 2019 271,705 people aged 17-34 registered to give blood – of which 175,233 were female and 96,472 were male.

3. Older people can and do regularly donate and save lives but overall they have higher prevalence of illnesses which prevent donation.

4. Field research by OnePoll of a representative sample of 1,000 men and women aged 18 and above, commissioned by Engine PR on behalf of NHSBT and conducted between 29 August and 12 September 2018.

5. Field research by OnePoll of a representative sample of 1,000 men and women aged 18 and above, commissioned by Engine PR on behalf of NHSBT and conducted between 29 August and 12 September 2018.

6. Figures recorded by NHSBT show between 1 September 2018 and 31 August 2019 people aged 17-34 gave 450,482 successful whole blood donations of a total 1,485,866. Amongst 17-34 year olds, 262,213 of the donations were from women and 188,269 from men.

18 October 2019

Organ donation: how have the laws in England changed and do you still have a choice?

New system could lead to additional 700 transplants each year by 2023.

By Sarah Young

The law surrounding organ donation in England has changed, meaning that most adults in the country will now have to 'opt-out' if they do not wish to be a donor.

It is hoped that the change will lead to an additional 700 transplants each year by 2023, and spark conversations around organ donation.

According to the NHS, nearly 4,000 transplants took place in 2018/19. However, there are currently around 6,000 people on the UK Transplant Waiting List and last year alone, more than 400 people died while waiting for a transplant.

Speaking of the new law, Anthony Clarkson, director of Organ and Tissue Donation and Transplantation, said: 'We are very pleased that Max and Keira's Law has passed its final round of parliamentary approval and we welcome the new legislation.

'We hope this law change will prompt all of us to consider whether or not we would want to donate our organs and encourage us all to register and share our decision with our family and friends. We will continue to provide the very best care and support to organ donors and their families, in order to help save more lives through the gift of organ donation.'

Health Secretary Matt Hancock agreed, adding that organ transplants are 'one of the modern miracles of science – helping offer hope in the midst of tragic loss.'

'Today we celebrate a milestone for organ donation as we move to a new system of deemed consent in England which will mean hundreds more lives could be transformed each year,' he said. 'I want to pay tribute to Max, Keira and everyone else who campaigned for this change.'

But, what exactly is an 'opt-out' system and why did the law need to change? Here is everything you need to know.

What is the new law around organ donation?

The law around organ donation in England has officially changed. As of 20 May 2020, all adults in England are now considered to have agreed to be an organ donor when they die unless they have recorded a decision not to donate or are in one of the excluded groups.

This is commonly referred to as an 'opt out' system. Previously, organ donation in England followed the 'opt in' rule, meaning that anyone who wanted to donate organs after they died needed to sign up as a donor on the NHS Organ Donor Register.

In Wales, the organ donation law is also 'opt out' and was introduced in December 2015.

In Scotland and Northern Ireland, the rules are 'opt in' for both organ and tissue donation. However, a version of an 'opt out' system is set to be introduced in Scotland next year, after the Scottish Parliament almost unanimously voted in favour of it.

In 2016, the Northern Ireland Assembly decided to keep organ donation laws as they are.

Why is the change referred to as Max and Keira's Law?

It is common for laws to be named after campaigners in recognition of their efforts to bring important issues to the attention of the public, hence why the new rules around organ donation are referred to as 'Max and Keira's Law'.

The name is in acknowledgement of all the campaigning Max Johnson and his family have done, both while Max was waiting for a heart transplant, and since he received the heart he needed.

Max's transplant came from a young girl called Keira Ball, who tragically passed away aged nine-years-old.

Why do we need an opt out system?

While there has been incredible progress in organ donation, there is still a shortage of donors. Last year, 408 patients died in the UK on the transplant waiting list.

According to the UK government, 80 per cent of people in England support organ donation but only 38 per cent had opted in under the old system, meaning families are often left with a difficult decision when a loved one dies.

It adds that less than half of families give consent for their loved one's organs to be donated if they are unaware of their wishes. When families know what their loved one would have wanted, they are much more likely to honour these wishes.

It is hoped that the new law will help to reduce the number of people waiting for a life-saving transplant.

Does the new law mean my organs will be automatically donated if I don't opt out?

No. The NHS states that your family will always be involved before donation takes place, but stresses that for this reason it is important that you choose whether you want to be a donor and discuss what you want to happen with your family, so your decision is clear.

Your faith and beliefs will also always be taken into consideration before organ donation goes ahead.

How do I opt out?

If you do not want to be an organ donor, you should record your decision on the NHS Organ Donor Register. The quickest and easiest way to do this is online, but if you don't have internet access you can call the contact centre on 0300 123 23 23.

If you opt out, you will be recording that you do not want to donate any of your organs or tissue, and opting out of donation completely.

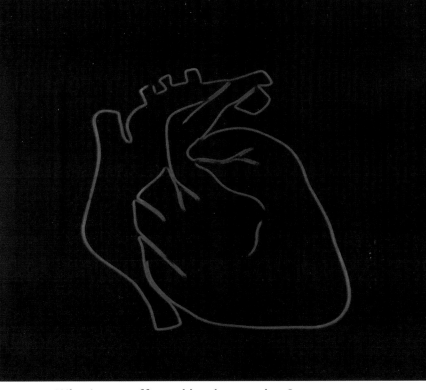

Who is not affected by the new law?

The opt out system does not apply to children under the age of 18 years old. In circumstances where a donation decision is required for someone under 18, the family will be asked to make that decision and provide consent, the NHS states.

Other people not included in the law change are those who lack the mental capacity to understand the new arrangements and take the necessary action, and anyone who has lived in England for less than 12 months.

Do I still need to register if I want to be a donor?

If you would like to be an organ donor, the best way to make sure your decision is honoured is to register as a donor and tell your family.

The NHS Organ Donor Register will be accessed by a specialist nurse prior to a conversation with your family to check if any donation decision has been recorded.

However, now that the new system has come into effect in England, if you have not expressed your decision to opt out of organ donation and are not in an excluded group, it will be considered that you consent to donate your organs.

Can I change my mind?

Yes. If you have recorded an organ donation decision on the NHS Organ Donor Register and want to change or reaffirm your decision, you can complete the 'amend your details' form or call 0300 123 23 23.

20 May 2020

How to get started with virtual volunteering

By Abigail Rooney

There's been a seismic shift in how we approach our daily routines due to current circumstances. Many of us have had to come to terms with the new normal, where everything from working to buying essentials to socialising has to be done over the internet. This includes the way we give back to the causes we care about or virtual volunteering. *Time* magazine notes that we are now online more than ever, with web use rocketing by as much as 35%. Luckily, the crisis isn't much of a deterrent to how we yearn to give back, as there are many opportunities available online that allow us to volunteer from the comfort of our own homes. Ross Britain previously highlighted how volunteering can do so much in inspiring people, and if you want to donate your time to a cause that is close to your heart, here's how you can get started with doing it virtually:

Do some research on volunteer programmes

As with anything, the key to success lies in being prepared. James Gonzales's tips for professionals working from home notes that since many of us have more time than we know what to do with, we can make productive use of it by being proactive and volunteering to do more. You may want to allot some extra time learning about the virtual volunteering programmes available, so you can make an informed decision on which cause or charity you want to focus on. You may opt to do more research on already established programmes like the United Nations and Red Cross, or you can find out more about lesser-known initiatives that could use a bit more support.

Share your personal story about a meaningful organisation

If you want to convince other people to do virtual volunteering without sounding preachy, you may want to share your personal story about how a meaningful organisation has changed your life. You never know, you might just touch someone's heart and persuade them to take action as well.

See if any local platforms speak to you, if not, come up with one

If there are smaller charities within your vicinity that may not have a formal virtual volunteer programme just yet, you can use this as an opportunity to lend a helping hand and assist them in setting one up. You may want to do research first about volunteer listings that are available in your area, but if nothing speaks to you, then you can reach out directly to the organisation you are interested in and ask them how you can be of help to them with the skills you have.

Use social media platforms for good

Many people are now spending more time on social media than ever before, so you may want to take this chance to leverage your network and spread the word about your organisation of choice. Operation Warm explains that spreading the word online about your favourite nonprofit charities is already considered volunteer work. You can opt to share important announcements from those organisations or you can craft your own posts to inform people about what they do.

Consider becoming a volunteer responder

You may also want to volunteer your time to help out organisations that directly give assistance to people in need of support during the pandemic. The Royal Voluntary Service has an ongoing programme that aims to supplement existing voluntary support within communities, take the burden off NHS services, and help people to stay healthy. There is a variety of volunteering options available. You're given the chance to choose whether you want to assist in collecting and delivering essential supplies, transporting patients to medical appointments, providing telephone support, and so much more. There is even an option to offer peer support, in which you'll be able to serve as a 'listening ear' to people currently struggling with the repercussions of COVID-19.

22 July 2020

How to get into volunteering

Right now, volunteering opportunities may not be quite the same as they used to be. But that doesn't mean you can't make a positive impact on the world!

Volunteering is a great way to pick up new skills and make a difference to a cause **YOU** feel passionate about. If you want to help out, here's a few things to aid you on your way

Choose your cause

Start with what matters most to you.

Feel strongly about environmental issues? Then roll up your sleeves and get stuck into one of the numerous conservation projects happening across the UK. Want to help out with some worldwide scientific research, from the comfort of your sofa? Check out Zooniverse. You can even volunteer with the things you love the most, like football.

There are lots of different areas to volunteer in, including:

♦ Mental health

♦ Environmental issues

♦ Poverty and homelessness

♦ Elderly

♦ Disabled people

♦ Animal welfare

Do your research

There are so many ways to help out, it's worth having a look at the sort of role you might be best suited to, the amount of time you're able to give, and what's safe to do during this time.

Do you like talking to people or would you prefer something less interactive? Do you feel at home helping out in a charity shop or want to be surrounded by nature? Organisations often need help in all sorts of areas. If you have a specific skill, you could offer your expertise too.

Online volunteering makes it easy to work with an organisation you care about that might be on the other side of the world. Projects could include helping with their social media, website, translations or writing articles, which all look awesome on your CV too.

Stay local

Once you've worked out what kind of volunteer you'd like to be, you can start by seeing what's available in your area.

Do-it.org provides volunteering opportunities by post code but you could always help people you know from a distance, support the vulnerable and lonely in your community, reach out to your neighbours, send care packages, or even set up a socially distanced bingo night for your street.

There are also a lot of community based groups online like Nextdoor, that you could sign up to (check with your parents first), keep up to date with, share information and be a positive part of your local community.

Volunteering doesn't have to be big, time-consuming or scary, you can be a micro-volunteer in all sorts of ways that fit around your life.

Go farther afield

Once lockdown restrictions have been lifted and we start to go back to a more 'normal' life (however that may be!), you may want to go on more of an adventure with your volunteering. So you could try 'voluntourism'. It's the perfect way to mix travel, with making a difference in a new community.

You can volunteer with various charities or NGOs (non-governmental organisations) including International Citizen Service (ICS), who work across the world making big changes at a local level.

Keep doing good

Even though we weren't able to be together on NCS this summer, we've got a new way for all of us to do some good together. Keep Doing Good - One Million Hours of Doing Good is our way of helping the country get back to business, once it's safe to do so.

All you have to do is make a pledge to donate some of your time through volunteering and social action. And by getting involved, you'll pick up new skills, help rebuild your local communities, create positive change and get all of our futures off to a good start.

1 June 2020

10 easy ways to be a more engaged citizen

By Ilona Lodewijckx

If you're reading this article, you're probably looking for a way to leave a mark on your local community. But it's easy to get sucked into the grind of everyday life.

When we're juggling work, school, hobbies, chores and family time, participating in your local government seems like a great idea in theory. But how do you possibly make time for it?

The good news is that participation doesn't have to be difficult or time-consuming. There are many things you can do as a citizen to uplift your community and the people in it. Some of them will cost you little to no effort, but with such a tangible impact on your neighbourhood, how could we ever call them 'small things'?

Let's take a look at different ways to get involved and leave your mark on politics and public life — without having to clear your calendar.

1. Stay up to date on (local) politics

Do you know who's in charge? Who has the decision-making power, and what are their plans for your community? Knowledge is power, so make sure to stay informed on what happens around you. Read the local newspaper or the town newsletter with your Sunday morning breakfast. Follow local politicians on social channels and, if you want, ask questions directly. Talk to your neighbours about the decision-making in your community and share your thoughts, or attend town meetings if you can find the time.

2. Volunteer in your community

Get your hands dirty if you can! Every small act of volunteering goes a long way. After all, you're directly impacting the existence of important organisations, charities and individuals in your city or municipality. It doesn't matter whether you're walking a shelter dog every weekend, signing an online petition about a local cause, or serving beers at the school's yearly fundraiser. A community is built on its active members, and volunteering now and then is a great way to make a difference.

3. Share your ideas and spark the debate

Is your city or municipality launching a digital citizen participation project? Great! That means that your administration is actively asking for your input. After all, who knows better what a community needs than its citizens?

On the platform, you can share your ideas, voice your concerns, and discuss local topics that matter to you, all without even having to leave the comfort of your own home. An added bonus? Participating on a digital platform gives you a clear and direct overview of the course that your administration is planning to take. Like we said, knowledge is power!

4. VOTE!

We get the chance to let our voices be heard every couple of years at the ballot box. It might not feel very impactful when you're checking the name or party of your choice, but the importance of casting your vote can't be understated.

Elections allow citizens to keep the administration accountable, and to weigh in on the direction and prioritisation of policy. Safe to say, getting informed and voting for your favourite candidate is one of the best ways to engage as a citizen.

5. Check your privilege and create space

Almost every person in this world is born with a certain amount of privilege. That means that they have a special advantage over certain other people or groups. Whether it's about ethnicity, social status, gender or physical ability, it's important to be aware of the privileges you hold, because if you use them in a powerful and positive way, you can truly transform society. Get informed on topics that don't affect you directly, and create space for voices that aren't heard as often in your community.

6. Scratch that cultural itch

Going to the library, visiting a local museum or heading to a concert isn't just fun and enriching, it's also beneficial for your community as a whole. Cultural organisations enable local people to read, write, and appreciate arts and music in an inclusive and accessible way. Getting a library card or buying museum tickets can really make a difference in the way these organisations function.

7. Settle down with a book

We told you engagement doesn't have to take a lot of effort, right? We weren't lying! Grab a drink of your choice, get settled in the cosiest nook you can find, and dive into an interesting book on politics or democracy. Don't know where to start? Take another look at our curated list of top 10 must-reads that'll inspire you to get involved. Not much of a bookworm? Check out these interesting podcasts or political documentaries!

8. Support local businesses

That cosy family bakery on the main square? The vegetable stand that's been selling leeks and carrots on the market for 25 years? The new coffee place across the street? For them, it makes a huge difference where you buy your croissants, zucchinis or latte macchiatos. Instead of shopping in bigger chains, try spending your hard-earned money at a local business. It'll make your community flourish!

9. Watch your ecological footprint

You don't want to live in a smoggy nightmare full of dirt and litter, and your neighbours don't, either. Keeping your community clean and healthy is an individual responsibility for everyone. Reduce the amount of useless plastic or non-recyclables you buy, see what you can re-use, and recycle the rest! Or maybe join #TrashTuesdays and take 10 minutes to pick up litter while you're out walking that shelter dog?

10. Take matters into your own hands

Agreed, this one takes a little more time and effort. But is there a certain topic that's close to your heart, and are you passionate about making a change? Then why not get started with your own citizen proposal? Gather the signatures you need and put your proposal on the council's agenda, join a group of like-minded peers, or why not join local politics? Become a member of a local party, help them with the campaigning in your city or municipality, or even get on the list yourself!

As citizens, we hold more power than we think. We can drastically change and improve our communities and the lives of the people in them if we put our minds to it. So let's get to work! How are you going to start?

8 November 2019

10 benefits of helping others

Volunteering your time, money, or energy to help others doesn't just make the world better–it also makes you better. Studies indicate that the very act of giving back to the community boosts your happiness, health, and sense of well-being.

Here are 10 benefits of lending a hand to those in need.

1. Helping others feels good

There is some evidence to suggest that when you help others, it can promote physiological changes in the brain linked with happiness. This heightened sense of well-being might be the by-product of being more physically active as a result of volunteering, or because it makes us more socially active.

2. It creates a sense of belonging

Helping others can help us to make new friends and connect with our community. Face-to-face activities such as volunteering at a food bank can also help reduce loneliness and isolation.

3. It gives you a sense of purpose

Studies show that volunteering enhances an individual's overall sense of purpose and identity. This is because helping others can make you feel rewarded, fulfilled and empowered.

4. Giving helps keep things in perspective

Helping others, especially those who are less fortunate than yourself, can help to put things into perspective and make you feel more positive about your own circumstances.

5. It's contagious

One study found that people are more likely to perform feats of generosity after observing another do the same. This effect can ripple throughout the community, inspiring dozens of individuals to make a difference.

6. Helping others can help you live longer

Regular volunteering can improve your ability to manage stress and stave off disease as well as increasing your sense of life satisfaction. This might be because volunteering alleviates loneliness and enhances our social lives.

7. It will give you a sense of renewal

Helping others can teach you to help yourself. If you've been through a tough experience or just have a case of the blues, the 'activism cure' is a great way to get back to feeling like yourself.

8. You'll boost your self-esteem

People who volunteer have been found to have higher self-esteem and overall wellbeing. The benefits of volunteering also depend on your consistency. So, the more regularly you volunteer, the more confidence you'll gain.

9. You'll create stronger friendships

When you help others, you give off positive vibes, which can rub off on peers and improve your friendships. Being a force for good in a friend's life can help build a lasting bond.

10. You become a glass half-full type person

Having a positive impact on someone else could help you change your own outlook and attitude. Experts say that performing acts of kindness boosts your mood and ultimately makes you more optimistic and positive.

28 April 2020

3 ways volunteering can boost your CV

Do you want to make a difference? If so, volunteering your time to a worthy cause is the perfect way to give back.

By Jade Phillips

People often associate this with giving but helping those less fortunate often has more benefits than you may think. When you invest your time in a charitable organisation and its mission, it's important that you pro-actively look for ways to make the most of the experience; especially as it's a great opportunity to learn and grow and looks great on your CV.

After all, it's not only paid experience that matters. If you're still not sure how offering your time can benefit you, here are three ways volunteering can boost your CV.

It proves that you want the experience

There's an ongoing problem that all job hunters come across at some stage: you need experience to get a job, but you need a job to get the experience. And the reality of this situation can leave people feeling defeated and weary about applying for certain positions.

However, if you're lacking experience, there are ample opportunities for you to get a taste of a new role by becoming a volunteer. Many people don't know that you can volunteer to be anything from a social media manager to a graphic designer or fund-raising manager.

By doing some unpaid work in a role that you're interested in, you're showing potential employers that you really want the job. This should help you to stand out from the crowd when applying for a role. However, if you want to make the most of your hard work, it's important that you can clearly show how your involvement has benefitted the organisation and its cause.

It can be pretty tricky to get a job when you have little experience, but volunteering provides you with the opportunity to change that. Not only is it a great way to give back, but it also gives you something relevant to boast about in your applications!

Volunteering gives an insight into your interests and your personality

Everything you choose to do outside of work gives employers an insight into what you really care about. As such, it's important that you support a cause that's meaningful to you when you volunteer.

As most employers only have your CV to figure out whether you're a good fit, you can include any charitable experience to help them see how well you fit into their culture. For example, a company that makes regular donations to charity or offers employees a chance to volunteer their time during working hours will see that you're a great fit. As a result, this is likely to give you an advantage over the competition.

It's not just your interests that employers look for when hiring new team members, it's also the type of personality you have, too. Taking part in volunteering is a great way to give a company a feel for your character and what you stand for. It doesn't just show that you like to give back, but it can also show leadership, intuition, determination and passion for a particular area.

It shows you're driven by more than money

Of course, any work you do as a volunteer will be unpaid, but this shouldn't matter. The fact you've put yourself forward to work without financial reward will show your dedication to the area your working in.

Everyone wants a job that allows them to maximise their skill set, connects to their passions and enables them to live comfortably. Job satisfaction comes from much more than your salary and volunteering proves that the work itself is what attracts you to the role.

Regardless of the sector, all employers want to hire people that have drive and can work to a high standard. So, by adding your volunteer experience to your CV, you can clearly show that making a difference means more to you.

Why volunteering can boost your CV

Overall, hiring managers will be looking for candidates that can demonstrate passion, determination and pro-activeness. Choosing to be a volunteer can help to prove all of these characteristics and then some.

Including this on your CV can be especially helpful if you don't have much experience to your name. Volunteering offers a lot of transferable skills that can translate to the workplace, from team work to leadership.

With all of this in mind, make sure that you highlight any relevant volunteer experience that you have on your CV. Remember to share the results that you were responsible for and relate it back to the objectives of your prospective employer so that your experience carries some extra weight.

6 March 2020

Key Facts

- Most people living in Britain say that they identify equally with their British and their national identity. (page 6)

- Those living in the North and the Midlands are more likely than those in the South to say they are more English than British. (page 6)

- 59 per cent of people admitted to having 'pride' in the British Empire. (page 8)

- Following the 2016 Brexit referendum, reports of hate crimes rose by 50 per cent. (page 8)

- Migrants continue to contribute more to the UK economy than they take out. (page 8)

- More than half of those over 60 see putting the kettle on in a crisis as typically British, compared to just 36 per cent of millennials. (page 10)

- 42 per cent of pensioners consider it British to be proud of where you are from, just 19 per cent of younger adults agree. (page 10)

- 78 per cent of Britons would describe themselves as being typically British. (page 10)

- 29 per cent of Britons do not feel they are able to show how proud they are of being British as much as they did before the Brexit referendum. (page 10)

- in 2017 the Saudi Arabian government made the unprecedented decision to grant a robot full citizenship of its country. (page 12)

- People aged 65–74 are the age group most likely to volunteer on a regular basis. (page 13)

- Women are more likely to volunteer at least once in the last year than men. (page 13)

- Around one in five people in employment volunteer regularly. (page 13)

- Volunteering rates are higher in rural areas. (page 13)

- People from higher socio-economic groups who live in less deprived areas are more likely to volunteer, but with smaller differences for informal volunteering. (page 13)

- More than a quarter of young people say they don't feel they belong in Britain. (page 18)

- 18-24 year olds account for less than 0.5% of all charity trustees, despite making up 12% of Britain's population. (page 18)

- Just 5% of adults think that young people today are very likely to take part in social action. (page 19)

- Young people who have taken part in meaningful social action were much more likely to believe they could have a positive impact than those who had rarely or never taken part in social action over the last 12 months. (page 19)

- 6 out of 10 young people have taken part in activities to help others and/or the environment. (page 20)

- Young people from lower-income backgrounds are significantly less likely to have taken part in meaningful social action than their wealthier peers. (page 20)

- Girls remain more likely than boys to participate, although the gap is small (40% for girls, compared with 37% for boys). (page 20)

- Those from more politically engaged households are considerably more likely to volunteer. (page 22)

- Fewer than 25% of under-35s will vote Conservative, compared to around 60% of their grandparents. (page 24)

- One in five UK adults (19%) has volunteered their time for community activities since the start of the lockdown on 23 March 2020. (page 25)

- The work this volunteer army is doing is estimated to have an equivalent economic value of more than £350 million a week. (page 25)

- Millennials – typically defined as those born between the early 1980s and the late 1990s or the start of the 2000s – were the least likely age group to volunteer. (page 25)

- More than three-quarters (78%) said they planned to continue helping those in need after the lockdown. (page 25)

- Women aged 17-34 are almost twice as likely to donate than men the same age, exposing the real need for more young men to donate blood. (page 30)

- One in five (20%) men in general admit they fear needles and one in four (24%) fear giving blood. (page 30)

- According to the NHS, nearly 4,000 transplants took place in 2018/19. (page 32)

- 80 per cent of people in England support organ donation but only 38 per cent had opted in under the old system. (page 33)

Activism

Campaigning to bring about political or social change.

BAME

An acronym which stands for Black, Asian and Minority Ethnic backgrounds.

Brexit

An abbreviation that stands for 'British exit'. Referring to the referendum that took place on 23 June 2016 where British citizens voted to exit the European Union. Britain left the EU on 31 January 2020, but a trade deal was finally reached on 24 December 2020.

Citizenship (education)

A citizen is an inhabitant of a city, town or country. The concept of citizenship indicates that a person feels as though they are a member of the society in which they live, and that they conduct themselves in a way that is responsible and respectful to fellow citizens.

Community

People living in one particular place or people who are considered a unit due to their shared values, beliefs or identity.

Ethnic minority

A group of people who are different in their ancestry, culture and traditions from the majority of the population.

European Union (EU)

The European Union (EU) is a group of countries whose governments work together to improve the way people live in Europe. It was formed in 1957, with just six members, and has grown to include 27 countries. In order to become members, countries are required to pay money (usually in the form of taxes) and agree to follow a set of rules/ guidelines.

Government

UK Government is responsible for managing the country. Our Government decides how our taxes are spent, and there are different departments that run different things: the Department of Health, the Department of Education, etc. UK Government is run by the political party with the greatest representation in the House of Commons and is led by the Prime Minister.

Hashtag (#)

The hashtag symbol (#) goes in front or a word or phrase to identify the topic of that message. This is commonly used on social networking sites, such as Twitter. On Twitter, when a hashtag rapidly becomes popular this is referred to as a `trending topic`.

Immigrant

A person living in a country to which they are not native. There are many social and cultural issues associated with immigration, particularly the integration of immigrants into the native population.

Nationalism

Nationalism is often considered to be more aggressive than patriotism, implying the desire to be a completely separate nation and intolerance of influences from other cultures. For example, a Welsh patriot might feel proud to be Welsh and love their country`s culture and values, but still be happy to be a part of the United Kingdom. A Welsh nationalist might feel that Wales should be separate from the UK, and feel intolerant of people or things from outside their country.

Organ/tissue donation

The process of a person choosing to donate their organs/ tissues for transplant. One donor can help several people because one person can donate a number of organs: kidneys, liver, heart, lungs, small bowel, pancreas, cornea (eye), bone, skin, heart valves, tendons and cartilage.

Patriotism

Feeling love and devotion towards your country and its values/beliefs.

Social action

Social action is about people coming together to help improve their lives and solve the problems that are important in their communities.

Statelessness

Statelessness refers to a lack of nationality, which can occur because of the redrawing of borders, or holes in nationality laws.

Volunteer

Someone who gives their own time to help other people.

Activities

Brainstorming

♦ What is citizenship?

♦ What is an 'active citizen'?

♦ What makes you a good citizen?

♦ What is 'civic duty'?

♦ List or create a mindmap of many different types of volunteering.

Research

♦ In pairs, create a questionnaire to find out whether people feel more British or nationalistic. Distribute your questionnaire to family and friends then write a brief summary of your findings. Include graphs to demonstrate your results.

♦ Research some volunteering schemes in your area and choose one you find particularly interesting. Create a short presentation about this scheme, aimed at persuading people to take part. Then perform your presentation for your class.

♦ Create a questionnaire to find out people's views on volunteering. Ask people if they volunteer currently, or plan to in the future. What types of volunteering would they like to do? Consider asking different age groups and see if the results differ.

♦ Do some research on different types of social action by young people. How effective have these campaigns been? Can you think of any ways they could be improved?

Design

♦ Design a poster to promote blood donation for young people.

♦ Choose an article from this topic and create an illustration to accompany it.

♦ Design a poster that shows the top ten things you believe to be 'typically' or 'quintessentially' British.

♦ Choose one of the articles in this book and create an infogram displaying the key themes and information of the article.

♦ Design a poster with some different volunteer schemes aimed at young people.

♦ Design a leaflet with benefits of volunteering. Include as much information as you can.

♦ Using the 'Top 40 signs of being British', create a poster to display some of the things that convey 'Britishness'.

Oral

♦ Choose one of the illustrations from this topic and, in pairs, discuss what you think the artist was trying to portray.

♦ In small groups, discuss the concept of 'British identity'. What kinds of things make you 'feel' British? Use the article 'The top 40 typically British traits, according to research' to help you

♦ What does it mean to be a 'responsible citizen'? Discuss in pairs.

♦ In small groups discuss communities. What do you think makes a community? What is community spirit?

♦ As a class, discuss the statement 'age is no limit to action'. Do you agree? If not, why?

Reading/writing

♦ Write definitions of the terms 'citizenship' and 'active citizen'.

♦ What does it mean to be a good citizen? Write 500 words exploring this question.

♦ Using the article '5 things councils should know about engaging young people, according to young people', write your own list of what you think can help improve engagement in social action for young people.

♦ Write a persuasive letter to your headteacher on either starting a social campaign, or a volunteer scheme to help your local community.

♦ Choose an article in this book and list three key points. Then write a one-paragraph summary of the article.

Acknowledgements

The publisher is grateful for permission to reproduce the material in this book. While every care has been taken to trace and acknowledge copyright, the publisher tenders its apology for any accidental infringement or where copyright has proved untraceable. The publisher would be pleased to come to a suitable arrangement in any such case with the rightful owner.

The material reproduced in ISSUES books is provided as an educational resource only. The views, opinions and information contained within reprinted material in ISSUES books do not necessarily represent those of Independence Educational Publishers and its employees.

Images

Cover image courtesy of iStock. All other images courtesy of Pixabay and Unsplash, except pages 1: jannoon028 from Freepik and 9, 17, 23, 32, 38 Rawpixel

Icons

Icons on pages 18 & 19 were made by Freepik from www.flaticon.com

Illustrations

Simon Kneebone: pages 2, 8 & 27.

Angelo Madrid: pages 4, 21 & 31.

Additional acknowledgements

With thanks to the Independence team: Shelley Baldry, Danielle Lobban, Jackie Staines and Jan Sunderland.

Tracy Biram

Cambridge, January 2021